CREATIVE QUILT COLLECTION
VOLUME ONE
FROM THAT PATCHWORK PLACE®

CREATIVE QUILT COLLECTION

Martingale® & COMPANY

FROM THAT PATCHWORK PLACE®

VOLUME ONE

Credits

President • *Nancy J. Martin*
CEO • *Daniel J. Martin*
VP and General Manager • *Tom Wierzbicki*
Publisher • *Jane Hamada*
Editorial Director • *Mary V. Green*
Managing Editor • *Tina Cook*
Technical Editor • *Laurie Bevan*
Copy Editor • *Ellen Balstad*
Design Director • *Stan Green*
Illustrators • *Laurel Strand and Robin Strobel*
Cover and Text Designer • *Trina Craig*
Photographer • *Brent Kane*

That Patchwork Place® is an imprint of Martingale &
Company®.

Creative Quilt Collection Volume One
© 2006 by Martingale & Company

Martingale & Company
20205 144th Avenue NE
Woodinville, WA 98072-8478 USA
www.martingale-pub.com

Printed in China
11 10 09 08 07 06   8 7 6 5 4 3 2 1

Mission Statement

Dedicated to providing quality products and service to inspire creativity.

Library of Congress Cataloging-in-Publication data is available upon request.

ISBN 1-56477-655-7

CONTENTS

INTRODUCTION

So many quilts, so little time! With today's quilt-shop shelves featuring an array of enticing books, it would take a lifetime to make all your favorite designs. That's why we've put together this sampling of patterns from our latest titles. Our *Creative Quilt Collection Volume I* contains 16 extraordinary quilts that offer a medley of styles and techniques. With the talents of so many topselling That Patchwork Place authors at your fingertips, you're sure to find inspiration time and time again!

Design. Whether your tastes are traditional, contemporary, or somewhere in between, you'll find patterns within these pages to keep you quilting. Scrappy stars, beautiful baskets, and gorgeous flowers are just some of the motifs you can choose from. Two doll quilts from the Civil War era are perfect for little-girl gifts. A flower-filled folk-art quilt makes a welcoming wall hanging for the foyer. Evelyn Sloppy, Rosemary Makhan, Joined at the Hip, and other popular designers offer unique creations for you to enjoy.

Fabric. No matter what kind of fabric your stash contains, you'll find a way to use it here! Florals, funky polka dots, classic calicoes, reproduction prints, and spring pastels are just a few of the fabrics to play with in this rainbow of colors and patterns. Instead of following fabric and color choices to the letter, use these patterns as a springboard to stretch your creativity—and your stash!—and truly make these quilts your own.

Technique. From beginner blocks to on-point wonders, you'll discover techniques in this collection of quilts to suit any skill level. Start with a technique you're familiar with—such as quick rotary cutting and strip piecing—then expand your skills with foundation piecing, hand appliqué, and dramatic borders. You'll find an especially fun method for using up leftover fabrics on page 88. Make the "Scotch Granny Quilt" first; then use the scraps from that project to make the charming "Scotch Granny Throw" on page 92.

Above all, have fun with your quiltmaking from start to finish. Whether you're stitching a quilt for a friend, for family, or just for yourself, you're sure to fall in love with several of these quilts. When you find one you like, be sure to check out the latest That Patchwork Place book from the quilt's designer. You may find that our *Creative Quilt Collection Volume I* will lead you to even more inspiration in your life-long quilting adventure.

ANNIVERSARY STARS

From *40 Fabulous Quick-Cut Quilts* by Evelyn Sloppy. Quilt made by Sharon Pennel.

Finished Quilt Size: 77½" x 95½"
Finished Block Size: 9" x 9"

Sharon worked on this warm and inviting quilt while on an anniversary trip with her husband. The quilt really shows off her talent for selecting fabrics and colors.

Materials

Yardage is based on 42"-wide fabric.

- 3¾ yards *total*, or 15 fat quarters, of assorted light fabrics for blocks
- 2¾ yards *total*, or 11 fat quarters, of assorted dark fabrics for blocks
- 1⅞ yards of floral print fabric for outer border
- 1 yard *total*, or 4 fat quarters, of assorted reds for the star points
- ¾ yard *total*, or 3 fat quarters, of assorted greens for the star points
- ¼ yard of red fabric for inner border
- ¾ yard of fabric for binding
- 5¾ yards of fabric for backing
- 81" x 99" piece of batting

Cutting

All measurements include ¼" seam allowances. Instructions are for cutting strips across the fabric width.

From the assorted reds for the star points, cut a *total* of:

- 40 squares, 4½" x 4½"

From the assorted light fabrics, cut a *total* of:

- 34 strips, 3½" x 21"; crosscut 7 strips into 32 squares, 3½" x 3½"
- 10 strips, 4" x 21"; crosscut into 48 squares, 4" x 4"
- 16 strips, 4½" x 21"; crosscut into 64 squares, 4½" x 4½". Cut 32 squares twice diagonally to yield 128 quarter-square triangles.*

From the assorted dark fabrics, cut a *total* of:

- 37 strips, 3½" x 21"; crosscut 7 strips into 32 squares, 3½" x 3½"
- 10 strips, 4" x 21"; crosscut into 48 squares, 4" x 4"

From the assorted greens, cut a *total* of:

- 24 squares, 4½" x 4½"

From the red fabric for the inner border, cut:

- 8 strips, 1½" x 42"

From the floral print, cut:

- 9 strips, 6½" x 42"

From the binding fabric, cut:

- 9 strips, 2½" x 42"

Before you cut, read the paragraph under "Making the Star Blocks" on page 11.

Making the Star Blocks

The cutting and piecing directions are written so that the inner backgrounds of the star-point units in the Star blocks will be the same fabric in each block. For a scrappy look, you can simply layer two red or green squares and two light squares in step 1 to make four triangle squares. Cut them into eight triangles and sew them together as in step 3. If you prefer this simpler approach, don't cut any of the 4½" light squares in half twice diagonally.

1. Referring to steps 1 and 2 of "Two Triangle Squares Method" on page 111, use a red 4½" square and a light 4½" square to make two triangle squares. Don't trim; cut them once diagonally to make four triangle units.

2. Using the same red fabric as in step 1, cut a 4½" square twice diagonally to make four quarter-square triangles. Using these red triangles and four assorted light triangles, sew the triangles together along their short sides into pairs as shown. Be sure that the red is on the left side on two pairs and on the right side on the remaining two pairs.

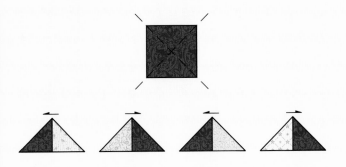

3. Sew together a triangle unit made in step 1 and a triangle unit made in step 2 to make a quarter-square-triangle unit; make four. Trim to 3½" square, referring to step 5 of "Two Triangle Squares Method."

4. Referring to "Triangle Squares" on page 110, use the 48 assorted light and 48 assorted dark 4" squares to make 96 triangle squares. Trim to 3½" square.

Make 96 total.

5. Using the four quarter-square-triangle units from step 3, three of the triangle squares made in step 4, and one light and one dark 3½" square, assemble the block as shown. The block should measure 9½" x 9½".

6. Repeat steps 1–5 to make a total of 20 blocks with red star points and 12 blocks with green star points. To make the green star points, you will use the green 4½" squares in place of the red squares in step 1.

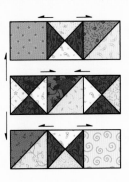

Making the Nine Patch Blocks

1. Sew together three of the 3½"-wide light strips along their long sides. Make a total of nine strip sets and press the seams as shown. Crosscut the strip sets into a total of 45 segments, 3½" wide; 30 should be pressed to the inside and 15 should be pressed to the outside.

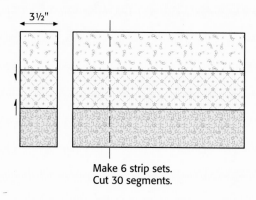

3½"

Make 6 strip sets.
Cut 30 segments.

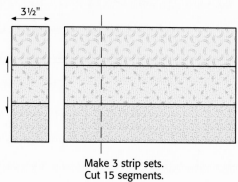

3½"

Make 3 strip sets.
Cut 15 segments.

2. Sew three segments together to complete a light Nine Patch block. The blocks should measure 9½" x 9½". Make 15 blocks.

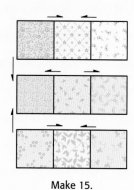

Make 15.

3. Using the 3½"-wide dark strips, make 10 strip sets in the same manner as step 1. Crosscut the strip sets into a total of 48 segments, 3½" wide; 32 should be pressed to the inside and 16 should be pressed to the outside.

4. Sew three segments together to complete a dark Nine Patch block. The blocks should measure 9½" x 9½". Make 16 blocks.

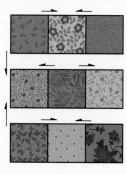

Make 16.

Assembling the Quilt Top

1. Sew the Star blocks and Nine Patch blocks together into rows as shown, paying close attention to the orientation of the Star blocks. Join the rows.

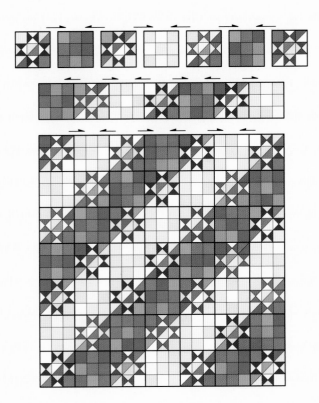

2. Referring to "Borders with Butted Corners" on page 117, attach the 1½"-wide red inner border and the 6½"-wide floral print outer border to the quilt top as shown above right.

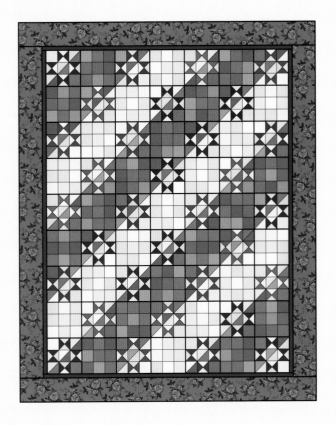

Finishing the Quilt

Refer to "Preparing to Quilt" on page 119, "Quilting Techniques" on page 120, and "Finishing Techniques" on page 121 for more detailed instructions, if needed.

1. Piece the quilt backing so that it is 4" to 6" longer and wider than the quilt top. Mark the quilt top if necessary. Layer the quilt top with batting and backing, and baste the layers together.

2. Hand or machine quilt as desired.

3. Trim the batting and backing even with the edges of the quilt top. Add a hanging sleeve if desired. Using the 2½"-wide binding strips, prepare the binding and sew it to the quilt. Make a label and attach it to your quilt.

From *Basket Bonanza* by Nancy Mahoney. Quilt pieced by Nancy Mahoney and quilted by Gretchen Engel.

Finished Quilt Size: 64½" x 64½"
Finished Block Size: 10" x 10"

The freshness of red, white, and blue never goes out of style.
The sawtooth border makes this wonderful traditional quilt particularly dramatic.
Nancy used a variety of blue prints in the baskets to create a scrappy look, and the cream
prints for the background provide a nice contrast for the bold reds and blues.

Materials

Yardage is based on 42"-wide fabric.

- 2⅛ yards of navy print for blocks, border, and binding
- 1⅞ yards of cream print A for blocks and sashing
- ⅞ yard of blue print A for blocks and setting triangles
- 1 fat eighth *each* of 7 cream prints for blocks
- ¾ yard of blue print B for blocks and sawtooth border
- ¾ yard of cream print B for blocks and sawtooth border
- 1 fat eighth *each* of 6 blue prints for blocks
- ⅝ yard of red print B for blocks and sashing squares
- ½ yard of red print A for blocks and inner border
- 4¼ yards of fabric for backing
- 68" x 68" piece of batting

Cutting

All measurements include ¼" seam allowances. Instructions are for cutting strips across the fabric width unless otherwise specified.

From blue print A, cut:

- 2 squares, 17⅜" x 17⅜"; cut twice diagonally to yield 8 side triangles
- 2 squares, 9¾" x 9¾"; cut once diagonally to yield 4 corner triangles
- 1 square, 7" x 7"

From *each* of the 6 blue print fat eighths, cut:

- 1 square, 7" x 7" (6 total)

From *each* of the 7 cream print fat eighths, cut:

- 1 square, 7" x 7" (7 total)

From red print B, cut:

- 2 squares, 9" x 9"
- 52 squares, 2½" x 2½"
- 12 squares, 1½" x 1½"

From cream print A, cut:

- 2 squares, 9" x 9"
- 12 strips, 1½" x 42"; crosscut into:
  - 12 rectangles, 1½" x 11½"
  - 24 rectangles, 1½" x 10½"
- 10 strips, 2½" x 42"; crosscut into:
  - 26 rectangles, 2½" x 6½"
  - 26 rectangles, 2½" x 4½"
  - 13 squares, 2½" x 2½"
- 7 squares, 4⅞" x 4⅞"; cut once diagonally to yield 14 half-square triangles. (You will use 13.)

From blue print B, cut:

- 8 squares, 10" x 10"

From cream print B, cut:

- 8 squares, 10" x 10"

From red print A, cut:

- 5 strips, 1½" x 42"
- 7 squares, 4⅞" x 4⅞"

From the navy print, cut on the *lengthwise* grain:

- 4 strips, 5½" x the length of fabric
- 4 strips, 2" x the length of fabric
- 7 squares, 4⅞" x 4⅞"
- 26 squares, 2½" x 2½"

Making the Basket Blocks

1. Pair each 7" blue square with a cream 7" square, right sides facing up; cut once diagonally.

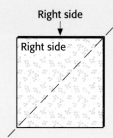

2. Using the first cut as a guide, cut 2½"-wide bias strips.

3. Separate and rearrange the strips, alternating the colors. You will have two sets of strips.

4. Sew the strips together along the bias edges, off-setting the point at the top edge ¼" as shown. Carefully press all seams toward the dark fabric. For the best results, press after sewing each seam.

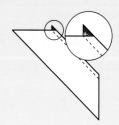

5. Make 14 strip sets. Cut 56 triangle squares, 2½" x 2½".

2½"

Make 14 strip sets.
Cut 56 units.

6. Repeat steps 1–4 using the 9" red print B squares and the 9" cream print A squares. Cut and piece 2½"-wide bias strips. Make 4 strip sets. Cut 26 triangle squares, 2½" x 2½".

2½"

Make 4 strip sets.
Cut 26 units.

7. Repeat steps 1–4 using the 10" blue print B squares and the 10" cream print B squares. Cut and piece 2½"-wide bias strips. Make 16 strip

sets. Cut 9 triangle squares for the blocks and 104 triangle squares for the sawtooth border, 2½" x 2½".

Make 16 strip sets.
Cut 113 units.

8. Draw a diagonal line from corner to corner on the wrong side of each 4⅞" red print A square. Place a marked red square on top of a 4⅞" navy square with right sides together, and stitch ¼" on each side of the drawn diagonal line; cut and press. This will make 14 triangle squares, 4½" x 4½". (You will use 13 squares.)

Make 13.

9. Draw a diagonal line on the wrong side of the 2½" red print B squares. Sew two 2½" red print B squares and one 2½" x 4½" cream print A rectangle together as shown to make a flying-geese unit; press. Make 26.

Make 26.

10. Sew a 2½" navy square to one end of a 2½" x 6½" cream print A rectangle to make a side unit. Press toward the navy square. Make 26.

Make 26.

11. Sew five triangle squares from steps 5 and 7 and one triangle square from step 8 into rows as shown; press. Sew the rows together and press. Make 13.

 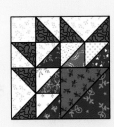

Make 13.

12. Sew two flying-geese units from step 9, two triangle squares from step 6, one 2½" cream print A square, and a unit from step 11 into rows as shown; press. Sew the rows together; press. Make 13.

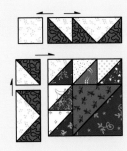 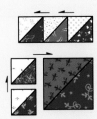

Make 13.

13. Sew two side units from step 10 and the unit from step 12 together as shown; press. Make 13.

 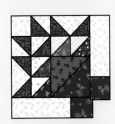

Make 13.

14. To trim the navy squares, align your ruler so that the 45° diagonal line is along the seam line and

the ¼" mark is on the crossed seams of the unit. Trim the excess fabric ¼" from the crossed seams.

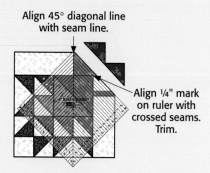

Align 45° diagonal line with seam line.

Align ¼" mark on ruler with crossed seams. Trim.

15. Fold a cream print A triangle in half and lightly press to mark the center of the long side. Sew a cream triangle to the unit from step 13, matching the center crease and the crossed seam to complete one block. Press toward the cream triangle. Make 13 blocks.

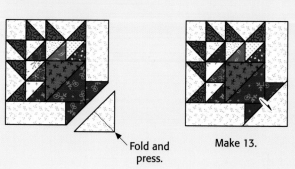

Fold and press.

Make 13.

Assembling the Quilt-Top Center

1. Lay out the Basket blocks, sashing strips, sashing squares, and 17⅜" blue side triangles in diagonal rows.

2. Sew the blocks, sashing strips, and side triangles together in rows, pressing toward the sashing strips.

3. Sew the sashing strips and sashing squares together in rows, pressing toward the sashing strips.

4. Sew all the rows together, pressing toward the sashing rows.

5. Add the blue 9¾" corner triangles last and press toward the triangles.

6. Square up the quilt top, trimming the edges ¼" from the corners of the blocks as needed. The quilt top should measure 48½" x 48½".

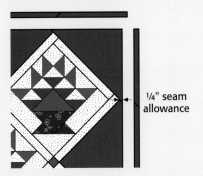

¼" seam allowance

Adding the Borders

Refer to "Borders with Butted Corners" on page 117 for more detailed instructions.

1. Attach the 1½"-wide red print A inner border to the quilt top. The quilt top should now measure 50½" x 50½" to fit the sawtooth border.

2. Sew 25 triangle squares from step 7 in "Making the Basket Blocks" together in a row as shown; press. Make four sawtooth rows.

Make 4.

3. Sew two of the sawtooth rows to the sides of the quilt top as shown. Press toward the red border.

4. Sew a triangle square to each end of the remaining two sawtooth rows as shown. Press the seam allowance toward the triangle squares. Sew the sawtooth rows to the top and bottom of the quilt top as shown. Press the seams toward the red border.

5. Attach the 5½"-wide navy print outer border to the quilt top.

Finishing the Quilt

Refer to "Preparing to Quilt" on page 119, "Quilting Techniques" on page 120, and "Finishing Techniques" on page 121 for more detailed instructions, if needed.

1. Piece the quilt backing so that it is 4" to 6" longer and wider than the quilt top. Mark the quilt top if necessary. Layer the quilt top with batting and backing, and baste the layers together.

2. Hand or machine quilt as desired.

3. Trim the batting and backing even with the edges of the quilt top. Add a hanging sleeve if desired. Using the 2"-wide navy print strips, prepare the binding and sew it to the quilt. Make a label and attach it to your quilt.

TRIANGLE SWIRLS

From *Log Cabin Quilts: A New Story* by Karen Murphy. Quilt made by Karen Murphy and quilted by Mary Decker.

Finished Quilt Size: 42¾" x 57"
Finished Block Size: 7¼" each side

There are no rules to say that the middle of the Log Cabin block has to be square! Instead of four walls, this Log Cabin block has only three. Shown here in the bright purples and greens of spring, this pattern will look terrific in almost any color scheme.

Materials

Yardage is based on 42"-wide fabric.

- 1⅜ yards of dark purple tone-on-tone for blocks, outer border, and binding
- 1⅛ yards of cream tone-on-tone for blocks and side and corner triangles
- 1 yard of dark green tone-on-tone for blocks and middle border
- ⅞ yard of dark blue tone-on-tone for blocks and inner border
- ¾ yard of light green tone-on-tone for blocks
- ⅝ yard of light purple tone-on-tone for blocks
- ⅝ yard of light blue tone-on-tone for blocks
- 3¼ yards of backing
- 54" x 68" piece of batting
- Freezer paper or template plastic
- Papers for foundation piecing

Cutting

All measurements include ¼" seam allowances. Instructions are for cutting strips across the fabric width. Small and large triangle patterns are on page 25.

From the light blue tone-on-tone, cut:
- 10 strips, 1½" x 42"; crosscut into:
  - 31 pieces, 1½" x 4" (block A, piece 2)
  - 31 pieces, 1½" x 6¾" (block B, piece 5)

From the light purple tone-on-tone, cut:
- 11 strips, 1½" x 42"; crosscut into:
  - 31 pieces, 1½" x 5" (block A, piece 3)
  - 31 pieces, 1½" x 7½" (block B, piece 6)

From the light green tone-on-tone, cut:
- 13 strips, 1½" x 42"; crosscut into:
  - 31 pieces, 1½" x 5¾" (block A, piece 4)
  - 31 pieces, 1½" x 8½" (block B, piece 7)

From the dark blue tone-on-tone, cut:
- 16 strips, 1½" x 42"; crosscut *10 strips* into:
  - 31 pieces 1½" x 6¾" (block A, piece 5)
  - 31 pieces, 1½" x 4" (block B, piece 2)

From the dark purple tone-on-tone, cut:
- 17 strips, 1½" x 42"; crosscut *11 strips* into:
  - 31 pieces, 1½" x 7½" (block A, piece 6)
  - 31 pieces, 1½" x 5" (block B, piece 3)
- 6 strips, 2½" x 42"

From the dark green tone-on-tone, cut:

♦ 19 strips, 1½" x 42"; crosscut *13 strips* into:

- 31 pieces, 1½" x 8½" (block A, piece 7)
- 31 pieces, 1½" x 5¾" (block B, piece 4)

From the cream tone-on-tone, cut:

♦ 5 strips, 3" x 42"; crosscut into 62 squares, 3" x 3" (block A, piece 1 and block B, piece 1)

♦ 3 strips, 6⅞" x 42"; crosscut into:

- 10 large triangles
- 8 small triangles
- 8 small triangles reversed

(Refer to the cutting layout below.)

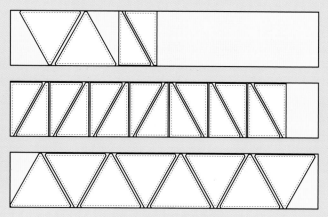

Cream fabric cutting layout

Making the Log Cabin Blocks

Refer to "Foundation Piecing" on page 111 for more detailed instructions.

1. Make 62 copies of the foundation-piecing pattern on page 24.

2. Paper piece 31 of block A and 31 of block B. In block A, the first round of logs is light-colored

and the second round of logs is dark-colored; in block B, the light and dark values are reversed.

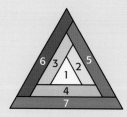

Block A.
Make 31.

Block B.
Make 31.

3. Trim the excess fabric from each block and remove the paper foundation.

Assembling the Quilt-Top Center

1. Arrange the blocks along with the large and small cream triangles according to the assembly diagram below.

2. Sew the blocks into rows, matching seams and corners, and press. Sew the rows together; press.

Adding the Borders

1. Sew the 1½" dark blue strips together end to end to make one long strip. Repeat with the 1½" dark purple and 1½" dark green strips. You will then have one long strip of each of the three different dark colors.

2. Sew the long edges of the strips together as shown to make a strip set. Press toward the dark purple.

Make 1 long strip set.

3. Referring to "Borders with Mitered Corners" on page 118, attach the pieced borders to the quilt top. When mitering the corners, be sure to match the seam intersections of each different border.

Finishing the Quilt

Refer to "Preparing to Quilt" on page 119, "Quilting Techniques" on page 120, and "Finishing Techniques" on page 121 for more detailed instructions, if needed.

1. Piece the quilt backing so that it is 4" to 6" longer and wider than the quilt top. Mark the quilt top if necessary. Layer the quilt top with batting and backing, and baste the layers together.

2. Hand or machine quilt as desired.

3. Trim the batting and backing even with the edges of the quilt top. Add a hanging sleeve if desired. Using the 2½"-wide dark purple strips, prepare the binding and sew it to the quilt. Make a label and attach it to your quilt.

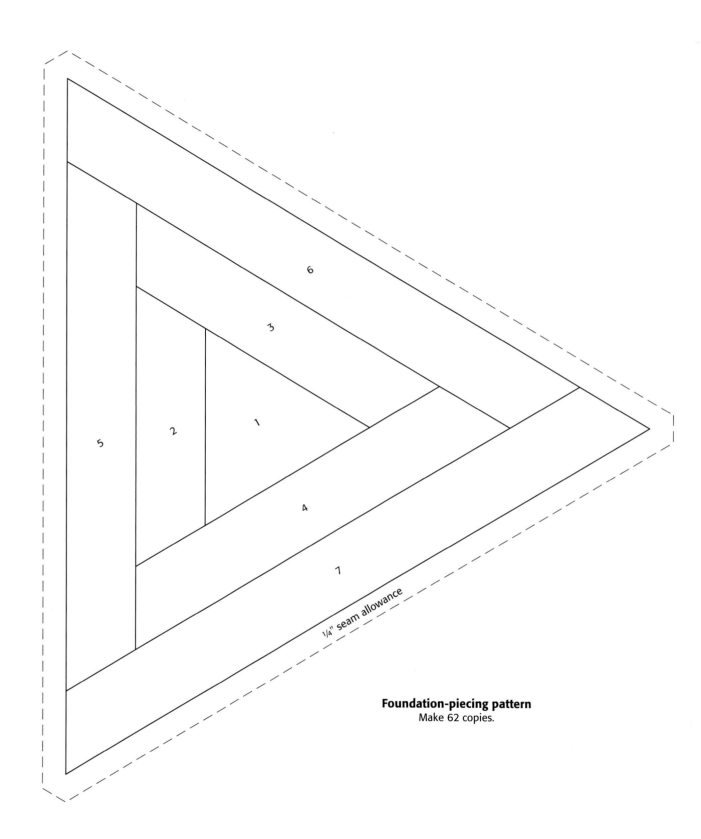

Foundation-piecing pattern
Make 62 copies.

1/4" seam allowance

6

3

5 2 1

4

7

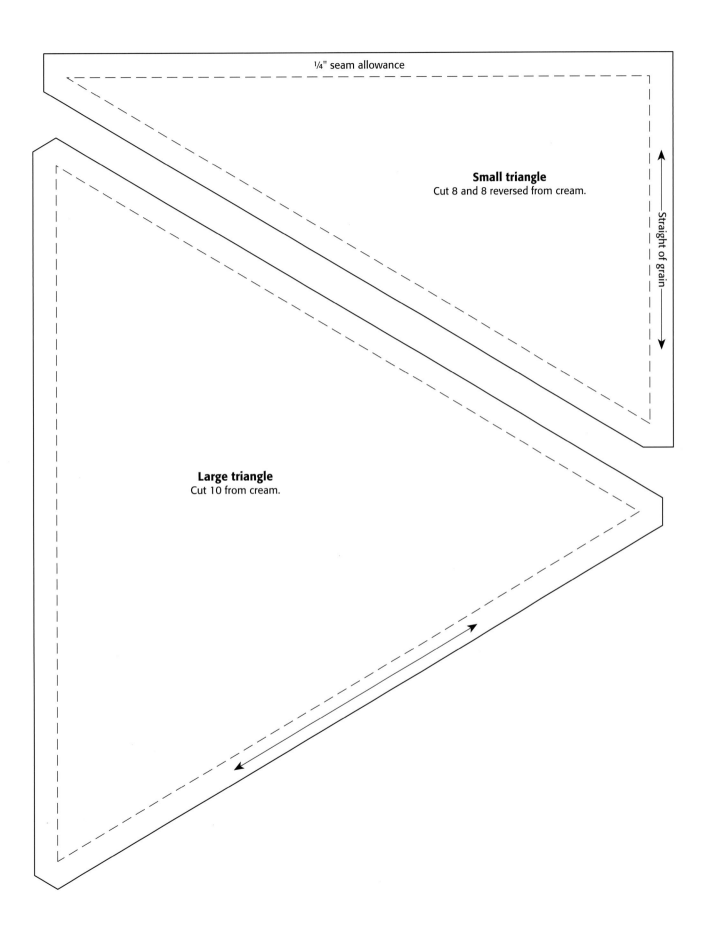

¼" seam allowance

Small triangle
Cut 8 and 8 reversed from cream.

Straight of grain

Large triangle
Cut 10 from cream.

INTERLOCKED MOSAIC STARS

From *Two-Block Appliqué Quilts* by Claudia Olson. Quilt designed by Claudia Olson, made by Linda Riesterer, and machine quilted by Jill Therriault.

Finished Quilt Size: 61" x 61"
Finished Block Size: 12" x 12"

This intriguing quilt is made with Interlocked Mosaic Arrows blocks and Eccentric Star blocks. Some of the mosaic blocks are modified to allow appliqué in the centers, creating Interlocked Mosaic blocks, while others are completely pieced. Additionally, by rotating the position of the Eccentric Star blocks in the quilt, they create either a light or dark frame around the adjacent appliqué blocks.

Materials

Yardage is based on 42"-wide fabric.

- 2½ yards of dark purple print for blocks, outer border, and binding
- 1¼ yards of navy blue print for blocks
- ⅝ yard of dark magenta print for star blocks and inner border
- ⅝ yard of gray print for star blocks
- ⅝ yard of white print for appliqué backgrounds
- ⅜ yard of multicolored print for star blocks
- ⅜ yard of lavender print for mosaic blocks
- ⅜ yard of light purple print for mosaic blocks
- ⅜ yard of teal print for star blocks
- ⅜ yard of medium purple print for mosaic blocks
- ¼ yard of medium magenta print for mosaic blocks
- Scraps of blue, purple, pink, maroon, and green fabrics for appliqué
- 3¾ yards of backing fabric
- 67" x 67" piece of batting

Cutting

All measurements include ¼" seam allowances. Instructions are for cutting strips across the fabric width.

Cutting for Eccentric Star Blocks

From the dark magenta print, cut:
- 2 strips, 5¼" x 42"; crosscut into 9 squares, 5¼" x 5¼"

From the teal print, cut:
- 2 strips, 5¼" x 42"; crosscut into 9 squares, 5¼" x 5¼"

From the dark purple print, cut:
- 3 strips, 4⅞" x 42"; crosscut into 18 squares, 4⅞" x 4⅞". Cut once diagonally to yield 36 half-square triangles.

From the gray print, cut:
- 1 strip, 6⅞" x 42"; crosscut into 2 squares, 6⅞" x 6⅞". Cut twice diagonally to yield 8 quarter-square triangles.
- 2 strips, 4⅞" x 42"; crosscut into 12 squares, 4⅞" x 4⅞"

From the navy blue print, cut:

- 1 strip, 6⅞" x 42"; crosscut into 4 squares, 6⅞" x 6⅞". Cut twice diagonally to yield 16 quarter-square triangles.
- 2 strips, 4⅞" x 42"; crosscut into 12 squares, 4⅞" x 4⅞"

From the multicolored print, cut:

- 1 strip, 6⅞" x 42"; crosscut into 2 squares, 6⅞" x 6⅞". Cut twice diagonally to yield 8 quarter-square triangles.
- 1 strip, 4½" x 42"; crosscut into 4 squares, 4½" x 4½". From the remainder of this strip, cut 2 squares, 3¾" x 3¾"; cut once diagonally to yield 4 half-square triangles.

Cutting for Interlocked Mosaic Blocks and Interlocked Mosaic Arrows Blocks

From the navy blue print, cut:

- 1 strip, 4⅞" x 42"; crosscut into 8 squares, 4⅞" x 4⅞"
- 1 strip, 2⅞" x 42"; crosscut into 10 squares, 2⅞" x 2⅞"
- 6 strips, 2½" x 42"; crosscut into 96 squares, 2½" x 2½"

From the white print, cut:

- 2 strips, 8½" x 42"; crosscut into 5 squares, 8½" x 8½"

From the medium purple print, cut:

- 2 strips, 4½" x 42"; crosscut into 20 rectangles, 2½" x 4½"

From the dark purple print, cut:

- 1 strip, 4⅞" x 42"; crosscut into 8 squares, 4⅞" x 4⅞"
- 2 strips, 4½" x 42"; crosscut into 20 rectangles, 2½" x 4½"
- 1 strip, 2⅞" x 42"; crosscut into 10 squares, 2⅞" x 2⅞"
- 2 strips, 2½" x 42"; crosscut into 32 squares, 2½" x 2½"

From the light purple print, cut:

- 1 strip, 5¼" x 42"; crosscut into 2 squares, 5¼" x 5¼"
- 1 strip, 4½" x 42"; crosscut into 8 rectangles, 2½" x 4½"

From the lavender print, cut:

- 1 strip, 5¼" x 42"; crosscut into 2 squares, 5¼" x 5¼"
- 1 strip, 4½" x 42"; crosscut into 8 rectangles, 2½" x 4½"

From the medium magenta print, cut:

- 1 strip, 4½" x 42"; crosscut into 16 rectangles, 2½" x 4½"

Cutting for Borders and Binding

From the dark magenta print, cut:

- 6 strips, 1½" x 42"

From the dark purple print, cut:

- 7 strips, 4¼" x 42"
- 7 strips, 2¼" x 42"

Making the Eccentric Star Blocks

You will need four full Eccentric Star blocks, eight half Eccentric Star blocks, and four corner Eccentric Star blocks for this quilt.

Full Blocks

1. Referring to "Quick Sew and Cut Method" on page 110, place a dark magenta square on a teal square. Sew to the right side of the drawn lines so that the teal triangles will be on the right side of each triangle pair. Cut and press as shown. Use 9 sets of squares to yield 36 triangle pairs.

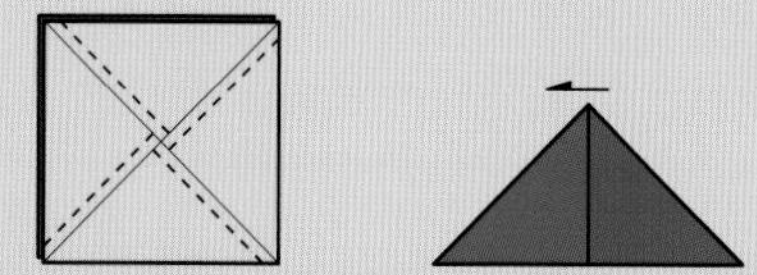

Make 36.

2. Sew the triangle pairs made in step 1 to a dark purple triangle as shown. Make 36 of these star-point units.

Make 36.

3. Referring to "Triangle Squares" on page 110, place a 4⅞" gray square on a 4⅞" navy square. Stitch, cut, and press as shown. Use 12 sets of squares to yield 24 triangle squares.

Make 24.

4. Lay out four star-point units from step 2, four triangle squares from step 3, and one 4½" multicolored square as shown, paying close attention to the color positioning for each unit. Sew the units together in rows, and then join the rows to complete an Eccentric Star block. Repeat to make a total of four blocks.

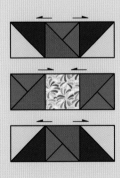 

Eccentric Star block.
Make 4.

Half Blocks

Pay close attention to color placement as you assemble the eight half blocks; you need four with the colors arranged one way and four arranged to create mirror-image units.

1. Using four of the leftover star-point units from step 2 of "Full Blocks," sew a gray quarter-square triangle and a multicolored quarter-square triangle to the dark purple sides of each star-point unit as shown. Make four.

   To another four of the remaining star-point units, sew a gray quarter-square triangle and a multicolored quarter-square triangle to the sides of each star-point unit as shown. Notice how the star-point unit is rotated and the placement of the multicolored and gray triangles has been reversed.

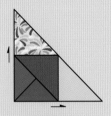 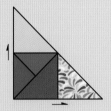

Make 4.   Make 4.

2. Sew the remaining navy/gray triangle squares from step 3 of "Full Blocks" to eight more of the star-point units as shown. Attach a navy quarter-square triangle to the opposite side of the star-point units as shown. Make four of each combination.

Make 4.

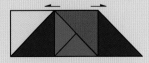

Make 4.

3. Sew the units from step 1 to those from step 2 as shown, taking care to match the color combinations correctly. Make four of each for a total of eight half blocks.

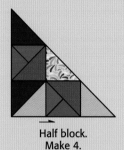

Half block.
Make 4.

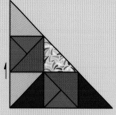

Mirror-image half block.
Make 4.

Corner Blocks

Using the remaining four star-point units, sew navy quarter-square triangles to opposite sides as shown, paying careful attention to color placement. Attach a multicolored half-square triangle to each unit to complete four corner blocks.

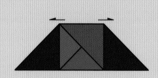

Corner block.
Make 4.

Making the Interlocked Mosaic Blocks and Interlocked Mosaic Arrows Blocks

This quilt uses five Interlocked Mosaic blocks with appliqué centers and four Interlocked Mosaic Arrows blocks.

Interlocked Mosaic Blocks with Appliqué Centers

1. Draw a diagonal line on the wrong side of 20 of the 2½" navy squares. Position a 2½" navy square on the corner of a white square. Stitch, trim to ¼" seam allowance, and press toward the triangle corner. Stitch a navy square to each of the remaining three corners. Make five of these units.

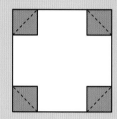
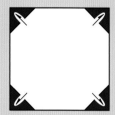

Make 5.

2. Draw a diagonal line on the wrong side of 40 of the 2½" navy squares. Sew a 2½" navy square to one corner of a medium purple rectangle. Repeat on the other end of the rectangle as shown to make a flying-geese unit. Make 20.

Make 20.

3. Draw a diagonal line on the wrong side of 20 of the 2½" navy squares. In the same manner as in step 2, sew a 2½" navy square to one end of a dark purple rectangle. Make 10 with the triangle on one end and 10 with the triangle on the opposite end as shown.

Make 10 each.

4. Using the technique for triangle squares described in "Triangle Squares" on page 110, place a 2⅞" navy square on a 2⅞" dark purple square. Stitch, trim to ¼" seam allowance, and press as shown. Use 10 sets of squares to yield 20 triangle squares. Sew one of these triangle squares to either side of 10 of the flying-geese units from step 2 as shown.

Make 20.

Make 10.

5. Lay out the various units for one block as shown. Sew the units together in rows, and then join the rows to complete one block. Repeat to make a total of five Interlocked Mosaic blocks.

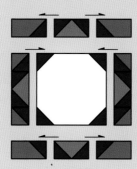 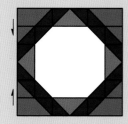

Interlocked Mosaic block.
Make 5.

6. Referring to "Appliqué Basics" on page 113, use the method of your choice to prepare the floral appliqués (patterns on pages 33–35). Appliqué one design on each block. Add embroidery according to the placement indicated on the individual flower patterns.

Interlocked Mosaic Arrows Blocks

1. Using the technique for triangle squares described in "Triangle Squares" on page 110, place a 4⅞" navy square on a 4⅞" dark purple square. Stitch, trim to ¼" seam allowance, and press as shown. Use eight sets of squares to yield 16 triangle squares.

Make 16.

2. Draw a diagonal line on the wrong side of the 16 remaining 2½" navy squares. Position a 2½" navy square on the dark purple corner of each triangle square from step 1. Stitch, trim to ¼" seam allowance, and press as shown. Make 16.

Make 16.

3. Using the quarter-square-triangle unit technique described in "Quick Sew and Cut Method" on page 110, position a light purple square on a lavender square. Sew to the right side of the drawn lines so that the lavender triangles will be on the right side of each triangle pair. Cut and press as shown. Use two sets of squares to yield eight triangle pairs. Join the triangle pairs as shown to make four quarter-square-triangle units.

Make 4.

4. Draw a diagonal line on the wrong side of the 2½" dark purple squares. Stitch a 2½" dark purple square to a medium magenta rectangle. Repeat on the other end of the rectangle to make a flying-geese unit. Make 16.

Make 16.

5. Sew a light purple rectangle to the bottom of half of the flying-geese units from step 4 and a lavender rectangle to the bottom of the remaining flying-geese units.

Make 8 each.

6. Lay out the various block units as shown, paying careful attention to color placement. Sew the units together in rows, and then join the rows. Repeat to make a total of four Interlocked Mosaic Arrows blocks.

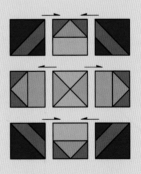 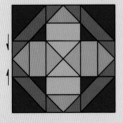

Interlocked Mosaic Arrows block.
Make 4.

Assembling the Quilt Top

1. Lay out the quilt blocks, half blocks, and corner blocks in diagonal rows as shown in the assembly diagram. Make sure all of the appliqué blocks are oriented in the same direction. Pay careful attention when placing the half blocks to complete the design as shown.

2. Sew the blocks together in rows, and then join the rows.

3. Referring to "Borders with Mitered Corners" on page 118, attach the 1½"-wide dark magenta inner border and the 4¼"-wide dark purple outer border to the quilt top. When mitering the corners, be sure to match the seam intersections of each different border.

Finishing the Quilt

Refer to "Preparing to Quilt" on page 119, "Quilting Techniques" on page 120, and "Finishing Techniques" on page 121 for more detailed instructions, if needed.

1. Piece the quilt backing so that it is 4" to 6" longer and wider than the quilt top. Mark the quilt top if necessary. Layer the quilt top with batting and backing, and baste the layers together.

2. Hand or machine quilt as desired.

3. Trim the batting and backing even with the edges of the quilt top. Add a hanging sleeve if desired. Using the 2¼"-wide dark purple strips, prepare the binding and sew it to the quilt. Make a label and attach it to your quilt.

Appliqué patterns
Enlarge patterns 133%.
Cut 1 of each piece.

Embroider details as indicated.

⊙   French knot

....   Stem stitch

—   Straight stitch

Appliqué patterns

Enlarge patterns 133%.
Cut 1 of each piece.

Embroider details as indicated.

⋰ French knot

······ Stem stitch

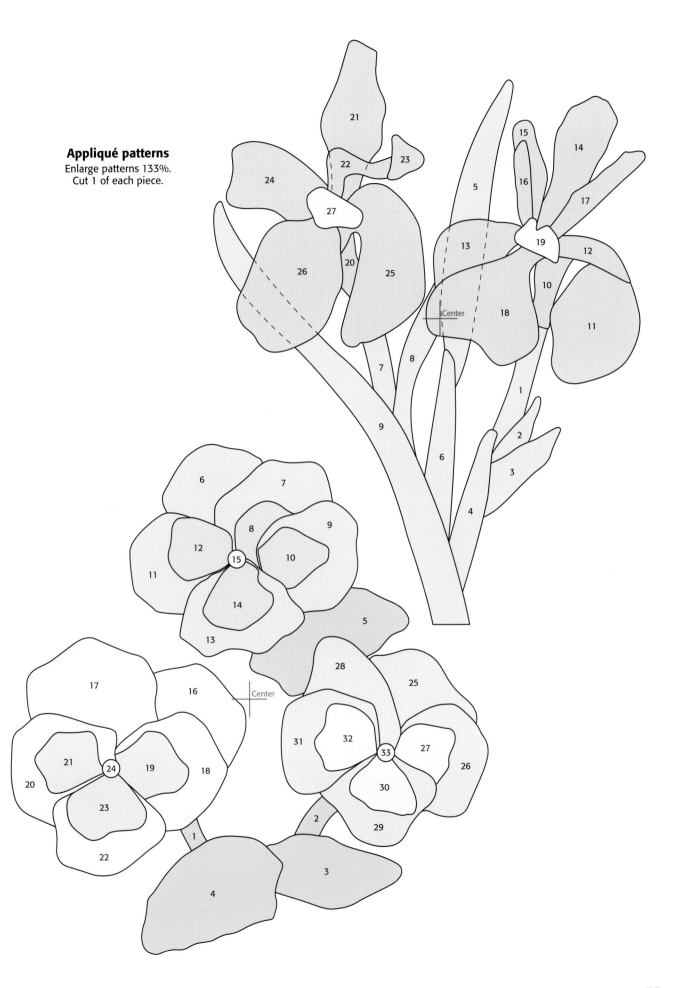

Appliqué patterns
Enlarge patterns 133%.
Cut 1 of each piece.

UNDERGROUND RAILROAD

From *American Doll Quilts* by Kathleen Tracy. Quilt made by Kathleen Tracy.

Finished Quilt Size: 19" x 25"
Finished Block Size: 6" x 6"

This doll quilt uses the traditional Underground Railroad pattern. This pattern may represent the network of safe houses for slaves on their journey to freedom in the years before the Civil War. Some say that secret messages were pieced in the cloth, while others disclaim the notion that quilts played any part in the movement. Even though this quilt is small, the pattern is an important tribute to the courage of those who changed history.

Materials

Yardage is based on 42"-wide fabric.

- ¼ yard of deep blue Civil War reproduction print for blocks
- ¼ yard of gold Civil War reproduction print for blocks
- ¼ yard of dark red check for inner border
- ¼ yard of medium blue fabric for outer border
- ¼ yard *total* assorted scraps of light and dark Civil War reproduction prints for blocks
- ¼ yard of brown fabric for binding
- ⅞ yard of backing fabric
- 22" x 28" piece of batting

Cutting

All measurements include ¼" seam allowances. Instructions are for cutting strips across the fabric width.

From the assorted light and dark Civil War prints, cut a *total* of:
- 48 squares, 2" x 2"

From the deep blue Civil War print, cut:
- 6 squares, 3⅞" x 3⅞"

From the gold Civil War print, cut:
- 6 squares, 3⅞" x 3⅞"

From the dark red check, cut:
- 2 strips, 1¼" x 42"; crosscut into:
  - 2 pieces, 1¼" x 12½"
  - 2 pieces, 1¼" x 20"

From the medium blue fabric, cut:
- 2 strips, 3" x 42"; crosscut into:
  - 2 pieces, 3" x 20"
  - 2 pieces, 3" x 19"

From the brown fabric, cut:
- 3 strips, 1⅜" x 42"

Making the Railroad Blocks

1. Randomly sew the light and dark 2" squares together into 12 four-patch units as shown, pressing the seam allowance of each pair in opposite directions. When joining pairs to make a four-patch unit, press the seam in either direction.

Make 12.

2. Layer each 3⅞" blue square with a 3⅞" gold square, right sides together, with the lighter square on top. Draw a diagonal line across each light square. Stitch ¼" from the line on both sides and cut on the drawn line. Press the seams toward the blue fabric.

Make 12.

3. Sew two triangle squares from step 2 and two four-patch units from step 1 together as shown, pressing the seam in each pair toward the four-patch unit. When joining the pairs, press the seam in either direction. Repeat to make a total of six Railroad blocks.

Make 3.

Make 3.

Assembling the Quilt Top

1. Arrange the blocks in three rows of two blocks each as shown to make the quilt center. Sew the blocks together into rows, and press the seams in opposite directions from row to row. Sew the rows together and press the seams in one direction.

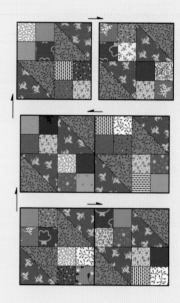

2. Sew the two 1¼" x 12½" checked pieces to the top and bottom of the quilt center, pressing the seam allowances toward the checked pieces. Sew the two 1¼" x 20" checked pieces to the sides, and then press again.

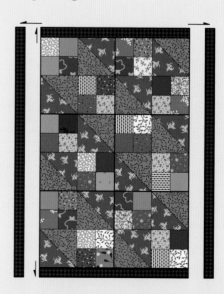

3. Sew the two 3" x 20" medium blue pieces to the sides of the quilt top as shown, pressing the seam allowances toward the outer border. Sew the two 3" x 19" medium blue pieces to the top and bottom of the quilt top, and then press again.

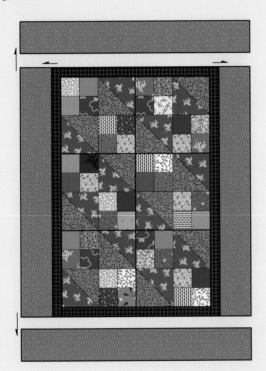

Finishing the Quilt

Refer to "Preparing to Quilt" on page 119, "Quilting Techniques" on page 120, and "Finishing Techniques" on page 121 for more detailed instructions, if needed.

1. Cut the quilt backing so that it is 2" to 4" longer and wider than the quilt top. Mark the quilt top if necessary. Layer the quilt top with batting and backing, and baste the layers together.

2. Hand or machine quilt as desired.

3. Trim the batting and backing even with the edges of the quilt top. Add a hanging sleeve if desired. Using the 1⅜"-wide brown strips, prepare a single-fold binding and sew it to the quilt. Make a label and attach it to your quilt.

CIVIL WAR NINE PATCH

From *American Doll Quilts* by Kathleen Tracy. Quilt made by Kathleen Tracy.

Finished Quilt Size: 18½" x 25½"
Finished Block Size: 6" x 6"

This doll quilt was made to look like a vintage quilt from America's Civil War era. The Civil War gave birth to some of history's most beautiful quilts. Quilts were made from scraps and sewed with a sense of urgency because they were so desperately needed for the soldiers. Children used their mothers' leftover bits to make small quilts like this for their dolls.

Materials

Yardage is based on 42"-wide fabric.

- ¼ yard of red print for borders
- ¼ yard of blue print for borders
- Scraps of 18 different dark or medium Civil War reproduction fabrics for blocks
- Scraps of 9 different light Civil War reproduction fabrics for blocks
- ¼ yard of gray fabric for binding
- ½ yard of backing fabric
- 22" x 29" piece of batting

Cutting

All measurements include ¼" seam allowances. Instructions are for cutting strips across the fabric width.

From *each* of the light Civil War fabrics, cut:

- 4 squares, 2" x 2" (36 squares total)

From 9 of the dark or medium Civil War fabrics, cut:

- 4 rectangles, 2" x 3½" (36 rectangles total)

From the *remaining* dark or medium Civil War fabrics, cut:

- 1 square, 3½" x 3½" (9 squares total)

From the red print, cut:

- 1 strip, 2½" x 42"; crosscut into 2 pieces, 2½" x 18½"

From the blue print, cut:

- 1 strip, 2" x 42"; crosscut into 2 pieces, 2" x 18½"

From the gray fabric, cut:

- 3 strips, 1⅜" x 42"

Making the Nine Patch Variation Blocks

Arrange four matching 2" light squares, four matching 2" x 3½" dark or medium rectangles, and one contrasting 3½" dark or medium square as shown. Sew the pieces into rows, pressing the seams of the top and bottom rows toward the corner squares and the seams of the middle row toward the center square. Sew the rows together and press the seams toward the center.

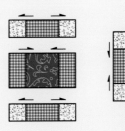

Make 9.

Assembling the Quilt Top

1. Arrange the blocks in three rows of three blocks each. Sew the blocks into rows, pressing the seams in the opposite direction from row to row. Sew the rows together and press the seams in one direction.

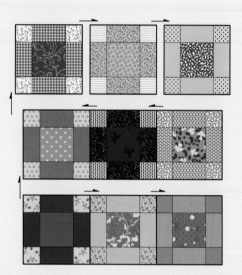

2. Sew the two 2½" x 18½" red pieces to the top and bottom of the quilt center and press toward the red border. Sew the two 2" x 18½" blue pieces to the red pieces and press toward the blue border.

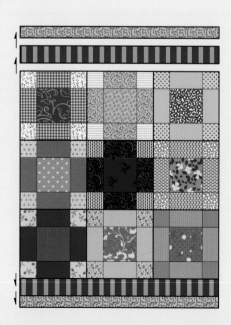

Finishing the Quilt

Refer to "Preparing to Quilt" on page 119, "Quilting Techniques" on page 120, and "Finishing Techniques" on page 121 for more detailed instructions, if needed.

1. Cut the quilt backing so that it is 2" to 4" longer and wider than the quilt top. Mark the quilt top if necessary. Layer the quilt top with batting and backing, and baste the layers together.

2. Hand or machine quilt as desired.

3. Trim the batting and backing even with the edges of the quilt top. Add a hanging sleeve if desired. Using the 1⅜"-wide gray strips, prepare a single-fold binding and sew it to the quilt. Make a label and attach it to your quilt.

ROAD TO PARADISE

From *More Biblical Quilt Blocks* by Rosemary Makhan. Quilt pieced by Rosemary Makhan and quilted by Sue Patten.

Finished Quilt Size: 63½" x 75½"
Finished Block Size: 12" x 12"

Using different fabrics in the corners of the Road to Paradise block creates a secondary pattern in between the stars. Choose a beautiful floral fabric for the borders and use this fabric as a guide when selecting fabrics for the blocks. Rosemary chose these fabrics because she imagines paradise as a beautiful sun-filled garden where the paths are strewn with rose petals. This quilt is bright and colorful but very soothing to the soul.

Materials

Yardage is based on 42"-wide fabric.

- 3½ yards of large-scale floral print for blocks, border, and binding
- 2¼ yards of small-scale floral background print for blocks
- 1¼ yards (1¾ yards for foundation piecing) of pink pin-dot fabric for blocks
- ⅝ yard of yellow-and-pink marbled fabric for blocks
- ⅜ yard of small-scale yellow print for blocks
- ⅜ yard of blue tone-on-tone print for blocks
- 4 yards of fabric for backing
- 67" x 79" piece of batting
- Papers for foundation piecing (optional)

Cutting

All measurements include ¼" seam allowances. Instructions are for cutting strips across the fabric width unless otherwise specified. The patterns for pieces A, B, and B reversed are on page 47. If you prefer to foundation piece the star-point units, follow the instructions that appear at the end of these cutting instructions.

From the yellow-and-pink marbled fabric, cut:
- 3 strips, 4⅞" x 42"; crosscut into 20 squares, 4⅞" x 4⅞". Cut once diagonally to yield 40 half-square triangles.

From the large-scale floral print, cut on the *lengthwise* grain:
- 2 strips, 8" x 68"
- 2 strips, 8" x 80"

From the *remaining* large-scale floral print, cut:
- 3 strips, 4⅞" x 42"; crosscut into 20 squares, 4⅞" x 4⅞". Cut once diagonally to yield 40 half-square triangles.
- 8 strips, 2¼" x 42"

From the small-scale yellow print, cut:
- 3 strips, 2⅞" x 42"; crosscut into 40 squares, 2⅞" x 2⅞". Cut once diagonally to yield 80 half-square triangles.

From the blue print, cut:
- 2 strips, 3⅜" x 42"; crosscut into 20 squares, 3⅜" x 3⅜"

From the small-scale floral background print, cut:

- 5 strips, 4⅞" x 42"; crosscut into 40 squares, 4⅞" x 4⅞". Cut once diagonally to yield 80 half-square triangles.
- 80 of triangle A*

From the pink pin-dot fabric, cut:

- 80 *each* of triangle B and B reversed*

If you prefer to foundation piece the star-point units, copy or trace the foundation-piecing pattern on page 47 onto paper. Make 80 foundation patterns. For piece 1, cut 80 squares, 5" x 5". For pieces 2 and 3, cut 80 rectangles from the pink pin-dot fabric, 3¾" x 5¾"; layer them in pairs, right sides together, and cut once diagonally. Half of the resulting triangles will be piece 2 and half will be piece 3. Refer to "Foundation Piecing" on page 111.

Making the Road to Paradise Blocks

1. Sew a yellow-and-pink marbled triangle to a small-scale floral triangle as shown; press. Make two for each block (40 total). In the same manner, sew the large-scale floral triangles to the remaining small-scale floral triangles; press. Make two for each block (40 total).

Make 40.

Make 40.

2. Sew the pink pin-dot B and B reversed pieces to opposite sides of the small-scale floral A pieces as shown; press. Or, foundation piece the star-point units using the foundation-piecing pattern on page 47 and referring to "Foundation Piecing" on page 111 as needed. Make four for each block (80 total).

Make 80.

3. Sew two small-scale yellow triangles to opposite sides of a blue square; press. Repeat on the remaining sides to complete the center unit. Make one for each block (20 total).

4. Sew all the completed units into three vertical rows as shown; press. Sew the rows together to complete the block. It is best to press the seams open when joining the units to make each block. This helps when sewing the blocks together because it distributes the bulk more evenly.

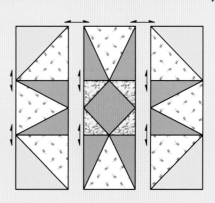

Assembling the Quilt Top

1. Lay out the blocks into five rows of four blocks each. Stitch the blocks together in vertical rows. Press the joining seams open.

2. Stitch the vertical rows together. Press the seams open.

3. Referring to "Borders with Mitered Corners" on page 118, attach the 8"-wide large-scale floral border strips to the quilt top.

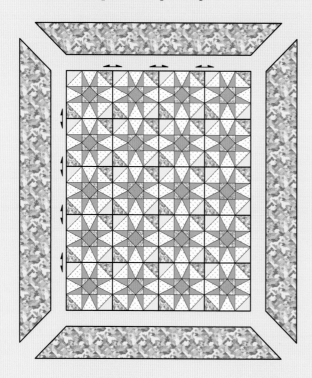

Finishing the Quilt

Refer to "Preparing to Quilt" on page 119, "Quilting Techniques" on page 120, and "Finishing Techniques" on page 121 for more detailed instructions, if needed.

1. Piece the quilt backing so that it is 4" to 6" longer and wider than the quilt top. Mark the quilt top if necessary. Layer the quilt top with batting and backing, and baste the layers together.

2. Hand or machine quilt as desired.

3. Trim the batting and backing even with the edges of the quilt top. Add a hanging sleeve if desired. Using the 2¼"-wide large-scale floral strips, prepare the binding and sew it to the quilt. Make a label and attach it to your quilt.

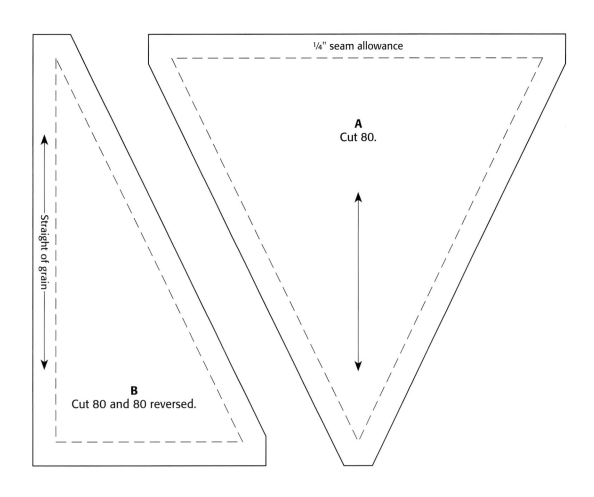

¼" seam allowance

A
Cut 80.

Straight of grain

B
Cut 80 and 80 reversed.

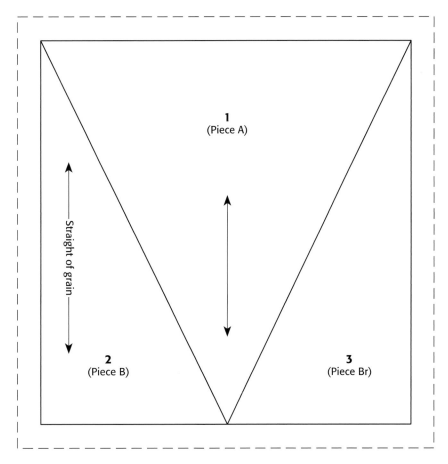

1
(Piece A)

Straight of grain

2
(Piece B)

3
(Piece Br)

Foundation-piecing pattern
Make 80 copies.

From *Alphabet Soup: Expressive Quilts with Folk-Art Flair* by Avis Shirer and Tammy Johnson. Quilt made by Avis Shirer.

Finished Quilt Size: 53½" x 35½"

You can never have enough flowers. The wagon is overflowing with beautiful blooms of every color that will brighten up any room of your house. What a wonderful quilt to welcome spring!

Materials

Yardage is based on 42"-wide fabric.

- 1¾ yards of blue-striped fabric for wagon background
- 1⅛ yards of light blue check for letter backgrounds
- ¾ yard of slate blue for letters
- ½ yard of green print for stems and leaves
- ¼ yard of brown print for wagon
- ¼ yard of mottled black for wagon wheels and handle
- ¼ yard of gray plaid for wagon tongue and wheel spokes
- ¼ yard *total* of assorted scraps for flowers in the following colors: 3 yellows, 3 purples, 3 reds, and 6 pinks
- ⅛ yard of yellowish green for flower centers
- ¼ yard of blue print for binding*
- 1⅞ yards of backing fabric
- 38" x 59" piece of batting

Yardage is sufficient for single-fold binding. Buy ⅛ yard extra for double-fold binding.

Cutting

All measurements include ¼" seam allowances. Instructions are for cutting strips across the fabric width unless otherwise specified.

From the blue-striped fabric, cut on the *lengthwise* grain:
- 1 strip, 17¼" x 53½"

From the slate blue, cut:
- Pieces needed for the words *(FRESH FLOWERS* and *PER BUNCH)*; see cutting and piecing instructions on pages 53–57
- 3 pieces, 1½" x 3½"
- 3 pieces, 1½" x 2½"
- 6 squares, 1½" x 1½"
- 1 piece, 1½" x 4½"

From the light blue check, cut on the *lengthwise* grain:
- 4 strips, 1½" x 53½"

From the *remaining* light blue check, cut:
- Pieces needed for the letter backgrounds *(FRESH FLOWERS* and *PER BUNCH)*; see cutting and piecing instructions on pages 53–57
- 11 squares, 1½" x 1½"
- 1 piece, 1½" x 2½"
- 1 piece, 1½" x 3½"
- 19 pieces, 1½" x 7½"
- 2 squares, 2½" x 2½"
- 4 pieces, 4½" x 7½"
- 1 piece, 3½" x 7½"

From the blue print, cut:
- 5 strips, 1½" x 42" (for *single-fold* binding)

Appliquéing the Center Panel

Fusible appliqué was used for everything except the stems, and each shape has a machine blanket-stitch around its edges to add a decorative touch. Refer to "Fusible Appliqué" on page 115 for detailed instructions. You may also use hand appliqué if you prefer (see "Appliqué Basics" on page 113). The appliqué patterns for this project are on pages 58–59. There is no pattern for the wagon; cut a rectangle 6" x 27" (this does not include the seam allowances) from the brown print fabric for this piece. Prepare all the shapes first so that you can work on the placement arrangement before anything is fused or stitched in place.

1. Place the wagon and wagon wheels on the 17½" x 53½" blue-striped piece. In the quilt shown, the wagon is placed 8" from the top edge of the background fabric and 3" from the bottom. It is also slightly off-center from side to side. It is approximately 12½" from the left edge and 14½" from the right edge. Don't fuse the shapes in place yet. Mark around the shapes with a chalk wheel or pencil so that you will know where to position the flowers, stems, and leaves.

2. Use the green print fabric to make ½"-wide bias stems, referring to "Making Bias Stems" on page 116. You'll need approximately 60" of stems.

3. There are seven groups of flowers in the wagon. Cut the bias stems in the following lengths, which include ¼" extra on each end for tucking under the wagon and flowers. Referring to the illustration on page 52 for placement, place them in order from left to right:

    Group 1: 3¼", 4¼", and 2¾"

    Group 2: 2", 4¼", and 1¾"

    Group 3: 1½" (this stem is tucked under the main stem) and 4¾"

Group 4: 2½", 4½", and 2"

Group 5: 4¾" and 2½" (this stem is tucked under the main stem)

Group 6: 2", 4½", and 1¾"

Group 7: 4", 3", and 2¾"

Placement can be tricky here so adjust the stems as necessary, making sure that they all fit into the wagon. When you are satisfied with the arrangement, appliqué the stems in place.

4. From the gray plaid, prepare a ¾" x 8¼" strip for the wagon tongue appliqué. Place the end that joins the wagon 1½" from the bottom edge of the wagon. Lay the handle on top for placement purposes and adjust as necessary. When the wagon tongue and handle placement is to your liking, appliqué both pieces.

5. Appliqué the wagon, followed by the wagon wheels, spokes, and wheel centers. Add the leaves and flowers.

Making the Letter Blocks

1. Piece the letter blocks needed for the words *FRESH FLOWERS* and *PER BUNCH*, referring to pages 53–57. Use the slate blue for the letters and the light blue check for the letter backgrounds.

2. To make the number 5, lay a 1½" slate blue square on top of a 2½" check square. Stitch diagonally across the small square. Trim to ¼" seam allowance and turn the resulting triangle over the seam and press. Repeat to make two of these units.

Make 2.

3. To one of the units from step 2, add a 1½" x 2½" slate blue piece to the top and a 1½" x 3½" slate blue piece to the left side. Press both seams toward the slate blue pieces.

Make 1.

4. Join a 1½" slate blue square to a 1½" check square. Sew this unit to the top of a 1½" x 2½" slate blue piece as shown. Sew this unit to the bottom of the remaining unit from step 2.

5. Sew 1½" check squares to each corner of a 1½" x 4½" slate blue piece, noting the stitching angles. Sew this unit to the right side of the unit from step 4.

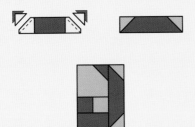

6. Join the unit from step 3 and the unit from step 5 to complete the number 5.

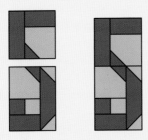

7. For the cent sign (¢), stitch two 1½" check squares to opposite sides of a 1½" slate blue square; make two. Also join a pair of 1½" x 2½" check and slate blue pieces, and a pair of 1½" check and slate blue squares as shown.

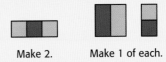

Make 2.   Make 1 of each.

8. Sew a 1½" check square to one end of two 1½" x 3½" slate blue pieces. Then to one of them, sew another check square to the opposite end, changing the direction of the diagonal.

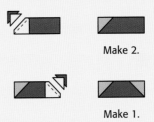

Make 2.

Make 1.

9. Stitch the units from steps 7 and 8 together as shown. Add a 1½" x 3½" check piece to the top of the unit to complete the cent sign (¢).

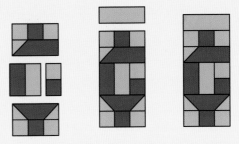

Assembling the Quilt Top

1. Assemble the top row of the quilt by sewing the letter blocks for *FRESH FLOWERS* together, separated by the 1½" x 7½" check strips and with a check strip at the beginning and end of the row. Between the two words, use a 4½" x 7½" check piece. To complete the row, sew a 1½" x 53½" check strip to the top and bottom of the unit. Press all seam allowances toward the check strips.

2. To make the bottom row of the quilt, sew the letter blocks for *5¢ PER BUNCH* together, separating the letters or symbols in each section with a 1½" x 7½" check strip. Then join the sections, separating them with the 4½" x 7½" check pieces. Add another of these 4½" x 7½" pieces to the right end of the row, and sew a 3½" x 7½" check piece to the left end of the row. To complete the row, sew a 1½" x 53½" check strip to the top and bottom of the unit. Press as before.

3. Join the letter rows to the top and bottom of the appliqué section. Press the seam allowances toward the appliqué.

Finishing the Quilt

Refer to "Preparing to Quilt" on page 119, "Quilting Techniques" on page 120, and "Finishing Techniques" on page 121 for more detailed instructions, if needed.

1. Cut the quilt backing so that it is 4" to 6" longer and wider than the quilt top. Mark the quilt top if necessary. Layer the quilt top with batting and backing, and baste the layers together.

2. Hand or machine quilt as desired.

3. Trim the batting and backing even with the edges of the quilt top. Add a hanging sleeve if desired. Using the blue print strips, prepare the binding and sew it to the quilt. Make a label and attach it to your quilt.

Cutting and Piecing the Letters

Letter F

From the letter fabric, cut:
A: 1 piece, 1½" x 7½"
B: 1 square, 1½" x 1½"
C: 1 piece, 1½" x 2½"

From the background fabric, cut:
D: 1 piece, 2½" x 3½"
E: 1 square, 2½" x 2½"
F: 1 square, 1½" x 1½"

1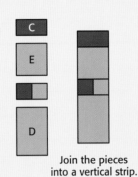
Make 1.

2
Join the pieces
into a vertical strip.

3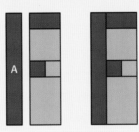
Join.

Letter R

From the letter fabric, cut:
A: 1 piece, 1¼" x 7½"
B: 1 piece, 1½ x 3½"
C: 3 pieces, 1½" x 2½"
D: 1 square, 1½" x 1½"

From the background fabric, cut:
E: 1 piece, 1½" x 3½"
F: 4 squares, 1½" x 1½"

1
Make 2.

Make 1.

2
Make 1 of each.

3
Join.

4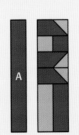
Join.

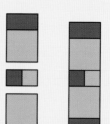

Letter E

From the letter fabric, cut:
A: 1 piece, 1½" x 7½"
B: 2 pieces, 1½" x 2½"
C: 1 square, 1½" x 1½"

From the background fabric, cut:
D: 2 squares, 2½" x 2½"
E: 1 square, 1½" x 1½"

1
Make 2.

2
Make 1.

3
Join the pieces into a vertical strip.

4
Join.

Letter S

From the letter fabric, cut:
A: 3 pieces, 1½" x 3½"
B: 1 piece, 1½" x 2½"
C: 4 squares, 1½" x 1½"

From the background fabric, cut:
D: 1 square, 2½" x 2½"
E: 1 piece, 1½" x 2½"
F: 8 squares, 1½" x 1½"

1
Make 2.

2
Make 1 of each.

3
Make 2.

4
Join.

5
Make 1.

6
Join.

7
Join.

Letter H

From the letter fabric, cut:
A: 2 pieces, 1½" x 7½"
B: 1 square, 1½" x 1½"

From the background fabric, cut:
C: 2 pieces, 1½" x 3½"

1
Make 1.

2
Join.

Letter L

From the letter fabric, cut:
A: 1 piece, 1½" x 7½"
B: 1 piece, 1½" x 2½"

From the background fabric, cut:
C: 1 piece, 2½" x 6½"

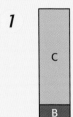

1   Make 1.

2   Join.

Letter O

From the letter fabric, cut:
A: 2 pieces, 1½" x 5½"
B: 2 pieces, 1½" x 3½"

From the background fabric, cut:
C: 1 piece, 1½" x 5½"
D: 4 squares, 1½" x 1½"

1
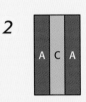
Make 2.

2

Make 1.

3

Join.

Letter W

From the letter fabric, cut:
A: 2 pieces, 1½" x 7½"
B: 1 square, 2½" x 2½"
C: 2 squares, 1½" x 1½"

From the background fabric, cut:
D: 1 piece, 2½" x 4½"
E: 1 piece, 1½" x 2½"
F: 4 squares, 1½" x 1½"

1
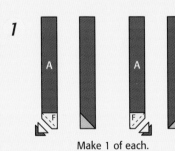
Make 1 of each.

2

Make 1.

3

Make 1.

4

Join.

5

Join.

Letter P

From the letter fabric, cut:

A: 1 piece, 1½" x 7½"

B: 2 pieces, 1½" x 2½"

C: 1 square, 1½" x 1½"

From the background fabric, cut:

D: 1 piece, 2½" x 4½"

E: 3 squares, 1½" x 1½"

1

Make 1 of each.

2

Make 1.

3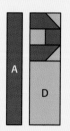

Join.

4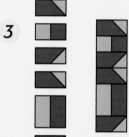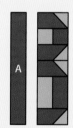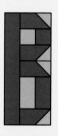

Join.

Letter B

From the letter fabric, cut:

A: 1 piece, 1½" x 7½"

B: 5 pieces, 1½" x 2½"

C: 1 square, 1½" x 1½"

From the background fabric, cut:

D: 1 piece, 1½" x 2½"

E: 5 squares, 1½" x 1½"

1 (diagrams)

Make 2 of each.

2 (E C and D B diagrams)

Make 1 of each.

3 (vertical strip diagrams)

Join the pieces into a vertical strip.

4 (diagrams with A)

Join.

Letter U

From the letter fabric, cut:

A: 2 pieces, 1½" x 6½"

B: 1 piece, 1½" x 3½"

From the background fabric, cut:

C: 1 piece, 1½" x 6½"

D: 2 squares, 1½" x 1½"

1

Make 1.

2 (A C A diagram)

Make 1.

3

Join.

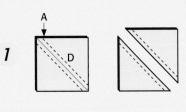

Letter N

From the letter fabric, cut:

A: 1 square, 3⅞" x 3⅞"

B: 1 piece, 1½" x 4½"

C: 2 pieces, 1⅞" x 3⅞"

From the background fabric, cut:

D: 1 square, 3⅞" x 3⅞"

Make 2.

Make 2.

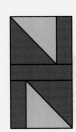

Join.

Letter C

From the letter fabric, cut:

A: 1 piece, 1½" x 5½"

B: 2 pieces, 1½" x 3½"

C: 2 squares, 1½" x 1½"

From the background fabric, cut:

D: 1 piece, 1½" x 5½"

E: 1 piece, 1½" x 3½"

F: 4 squares, 1½" x 1½"

Make 2.

Make 1.

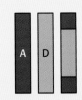

Join.

Join.

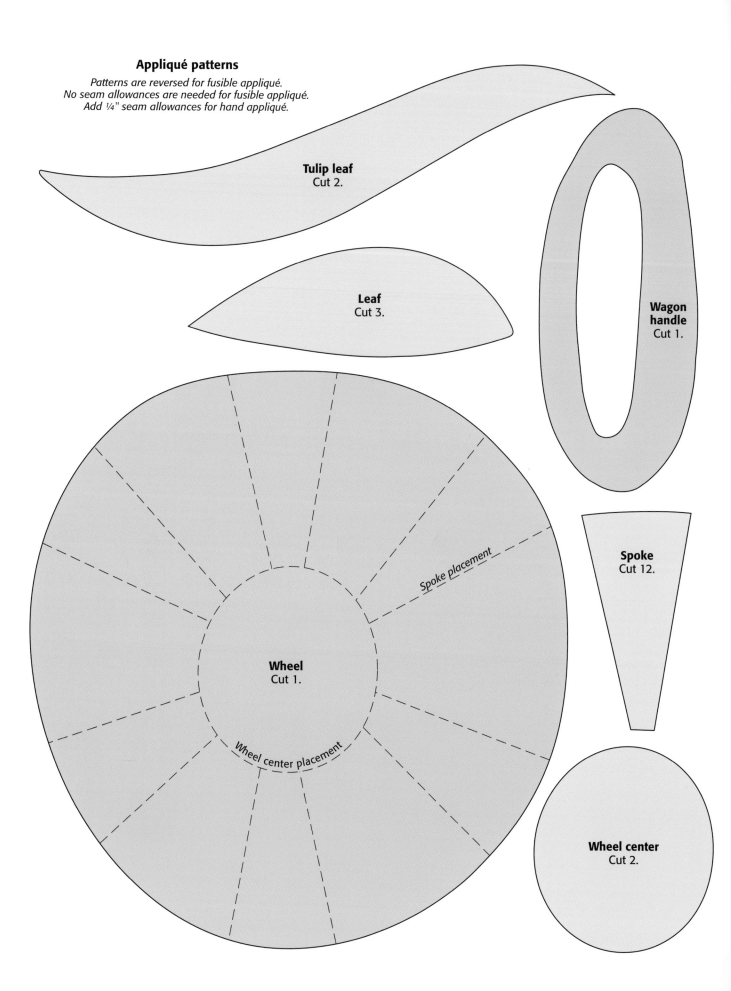

Appliqué patterns

Patterns are reversed for fusible appliqué.
No seam allowances are needed for fusible appliqué.
Add ¼" seam allowances for hand appliqué.

Tulip leaf
Cut 2.

Leaf
Cut 3.

Wagon handle
Cut 1.

Spoke
Cut 12.

Wheel
Cut 1.

Spoke placement

Wheel center placement

Wheel center
Cut 2.

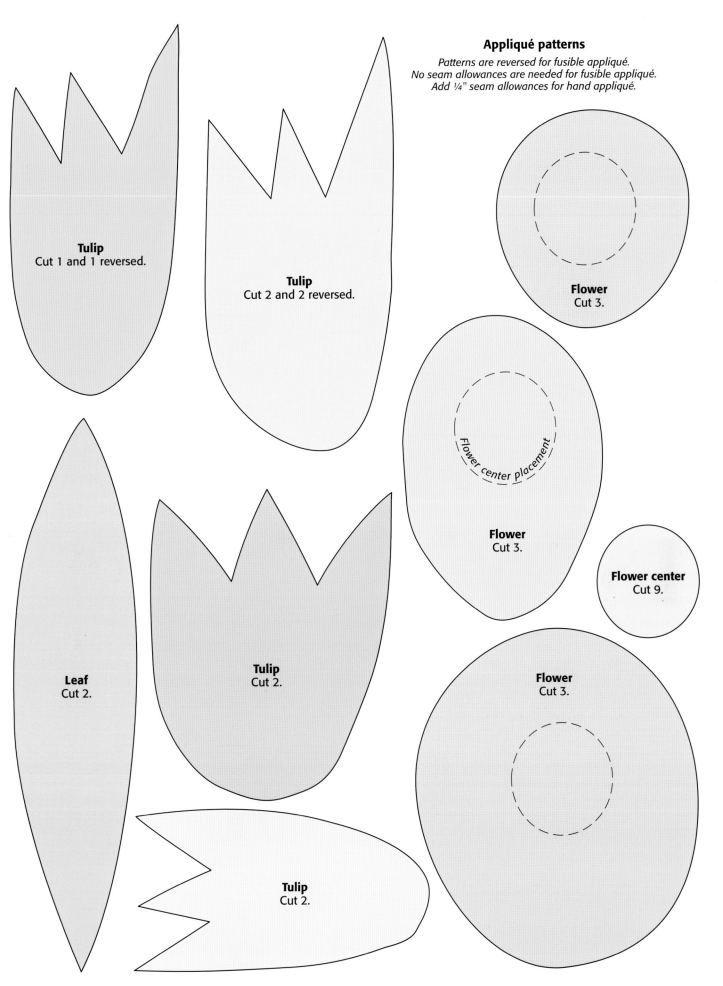

Appliqué patterns

Patterns are reversed for fusible appliqué.
No seam allowances are needed for fusible appliqué.
Add ¼" seam allowances for hand appliqué.

Tulip
Cut 1 and 1 reversed.

Tulip
Cut 2 and 2 reversed.

Flower
Cut 3.

Flower center placement

Flower
Cut 3.

Flower center
Cut 9.

Leaf
Cut 2.

Tulip
Cut 2.

Tulip
Cut 2.

Flower
Cut 3.

SWEET DREAMS

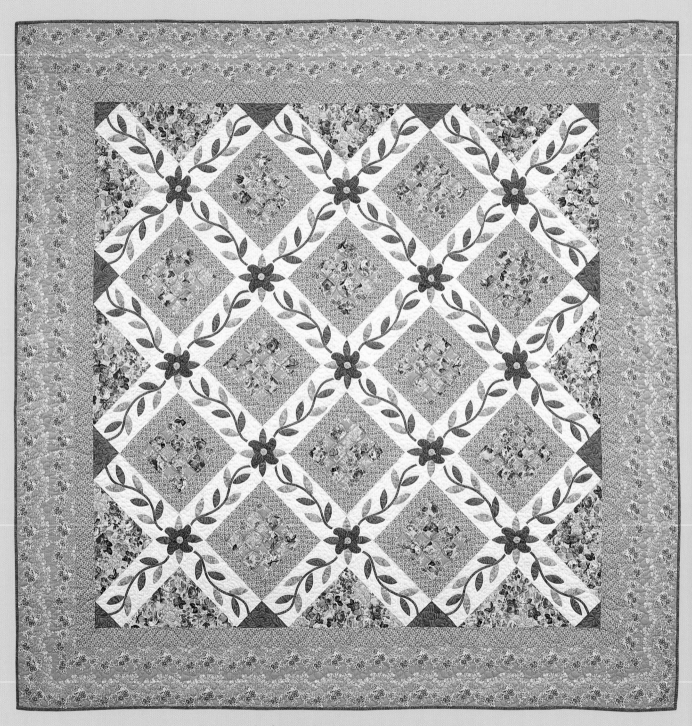

From *Tea in the Garden* by Cynthia Tomaszewski.
Quilt designed and pieced by Cynthia Tomaszewski, and machine quilted by Donna Ward.

Finished Quilt Size: 71½" x 71½"
Finished Block Size: 9" x 9"

Old-fashioned floral fabrics make a striking backdrop for these flowing vines.
Use traditional hand appliqué or fusible appliqué and embellish
with shimmering threads and cheerful buttons.

Materials

Yardage is based on 42"-wide fabric.

- 2⅜ yards of large-scale blue floral print for blocks and outer border
- 2⅛ yards of small-scale red-and-beige print for blocks and inner border
- 1⅝ yards of white-on-cream print for sashing
- 1⅜ yards of beige floral print for blocks and setting triangles
- 1¼ yards of green print A for leaves, bias stems, and sashing triangles
- ¾ yard of green print B for leaves
- ⅜ yard of red print B for flowers
- ⅝ yard of red print A for binding
- 4⅝ yards of fabric for backing
- 78" x 78" piece of batting
- 13 buttons, ¾" diameter, for flower centers (optional)

Cutting

All measurements include ¼" seam allowances. Instructions are for cutting strips across the fabric width unless otherwise specified.

From green print A, cut:

- ¾"-wide bias strips to measure a total of 432"
- 2 squares, 3¾" x 3¾"; cut once diagonally to yield 4 half-square triangles
- 2 squares, 7" x 7"; cut twice diagonally to yield 8 quarter-square triangles

From the beige floral print, cut:

- 6 strips, 2" x 42"
- 3 squares, 14" x 14"; cut twice diagonally to yield 12 side triangles

From the red-and-beige print, cut on the *lengthwise* grain:

- 4 strips, 2½" x approximately 65"
- 6 strips, 2" x length of fabric; crosscut into:
  - 24 pieces, 2" x 9½"
  - 24 pieces, 2" x 6½"

From red print A, cut:

- 8 strips, 2" x 42"

From the white-on-cream print, cut*:

◆ 11 strips, 4½" x 42"; crosscut into:
  · 36 pieces, 4½" x 9½"
  · 13 squares, 4½" x 4½"

From the blue floral print, cut on the *lengthwise* grain:

◆ 4 strips, 6½" x approximately 77"**

◆ 3 strips, 2" x length of fabric; crosscut each strip once across the grain. You should now have 6 strips, 2" x approximately 42".

If you're working with fabric that tends to unravel, you may cut the dimensions of these pieces 1" larger and, after completing your appliqué, trim them to the required size.

**If your print has a directional design or stripe as this project's does, you will need to cut the borders following the design so that each strip is the same. The pattern needs to meet at the mitered corners.*

Appliquéing the Sashing Strips and Squares

Refer to "Appliqué Basics" on page 113 for more detailed instructions.

1. Refer to "Making Bias Stems" on page 116 to make ¼"-wide bias stems from the green print A bias strips. Using the appliqué placement guide on page 64, position and pin the stems in place on the 4½" x 9½" white-on-cream sashing strips. Appliqué the stems in place using your favorite method.

2. Make appliqué templates for the leaves and flowers by tracing the patterns on pages 64–65. Cut out the number of each shape indicated on the patterns.

3. Appliqué all the leaves and flowers to the white-on-cream 4½" x 9½" sashing strips and 4½" squares.

Making the Sixteen Patch Blocks

1. Sew the 2"-wide strips of beige floral and blue floral together in groups of four to form strip sets. Make three sets and press the seams in one direction. From the strip sets, cut a total of 48 segments, 2" wide.

Make 3 strip sets.
Cut 48 segments.

2. Sew four of the segments from step 1 together as shown. Press the seams in one direction. Make 12 of these units.

Make 12.

3. Add the 2" x 6½" red-and-beige pieces to the top and bottom of each unit from step 2; press. Add the 2" x 9½" pieces to the sides of each unit and press. The block should measure 9½" x 9½". Make 12.

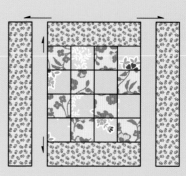

Make 12.

Assembling the Quilt Top

1. Assemble the appliqué sashing strips and squares, Sixteen Patch blocks, sashing triangles, and side triangles into diagonal rows as shown in the assembly diagram below. Sew the pieces together into rows and press seams toward the darker fabric when possible. Sew the rows together. Press the seams in one direction.

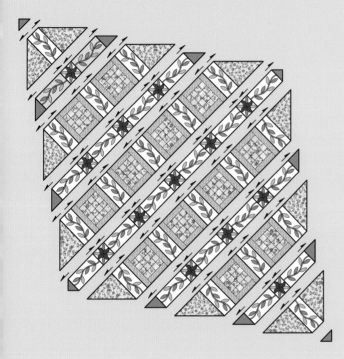

2. Referring to "Borders with Mitered Corners" on page 118, attach the 2½"-wide red-and-beige inner border and the 6½"-wide blue floral outer border to the quilt top. When mitering the corners, be sure to match the seam intersections of each different border.

Finishing the Quilt

Refer to "Preparing to Quilt" on page 119, "Quilting Techniques" on page 120, and "Finishing Techniques" on page 121 for more detailed instructions, if needed.

1. Piece the quilt backing so that it is 4" to 6" longer and wider than the quilt top. Mark the quilt top if necessary. Layer the quilt top with batting and backing, and baste the layers together.

2. Hand or machine quilt as desired.

3. Trim the batting and backing even with the edges of the quilt top. Add a hanging sleeve if desired. Using the 2"-wide red print A strips, prepare the binding and sew it to the quilt. Make a label and attach it to your quilt.

4. Sew buttons to the flower centers, if desired.

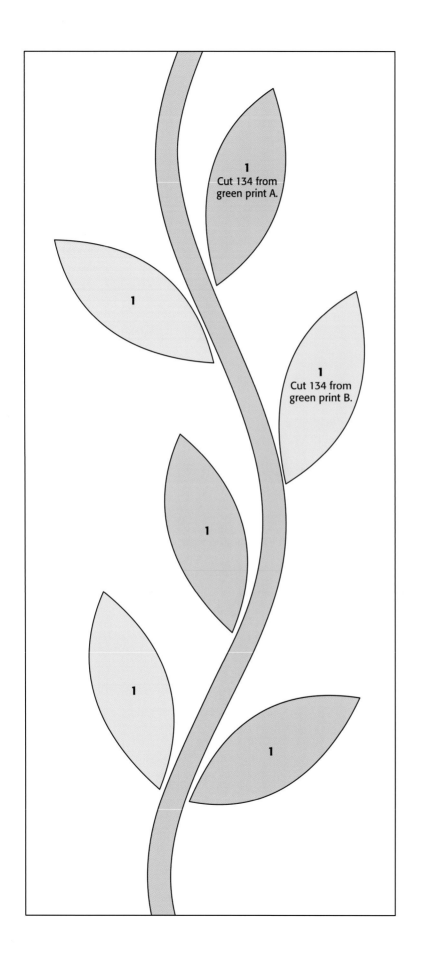

1
Cut 134 from
green print A.

1

1
Cut 134 from
green print B.

1

1

1

**Appliqué patterns and
placement guide**

**Appliqué patterns and
placement guide**

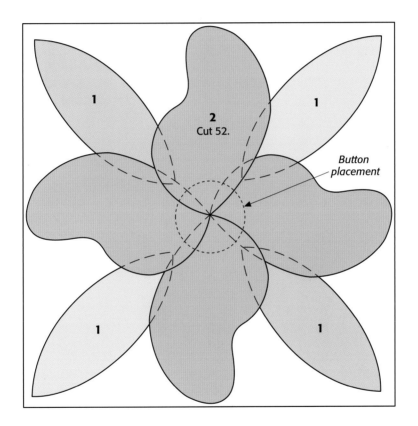

1

2
Cut 52.

1

*Button
placement*

1

1

BRIGHT BOUQUETS

By Laurie Bevan, author of *Lickety-Split Quilts.* Quilt pieced by Laurie Bevan and machine quilted by Karen Ford.

Finished Quilt Size: 68⅜" x 68⅜"
Finished Block Size: 16" x 16"

Bring springtime indoors with this flowery quilt. Finish it
lickety-split using big blocks; then head outdoors to enjoy your own garden.

Materials

Yardage is based on 42"-wide fabric.

- 4 yards of pale yellow floral for blocks and setting triangles
- ¾ yard of green print for blocks
- ½ yard of blue print for blocks
- ½ yard of pink print for blocks
- ½ yard of orange print for blocks
- ½ yard of purple print for blocks
- ½ yard of pink print for binding
- 4½ yards of fabric for backing
- 74" x 74" piece of batting

Cutting

All measurements include ¼" seam allowances. Instructions are for cutting strips across the fabric width.

From the pink print for blocks, cut:
- 2 strips, 4½" x 42"; crosscut into 13 squares, 4½" x 4½"
- 1 strip, 4⅞" x 42"; crosscut into 7 squares, 4⅞" x 4⅞"

From the blue print, cut:
- 2 strips, 4½" x 42"; crosscut into 13 squares, 4½" x 4½"
- 1 strip, 4⅞" x 42"; crosscut into 7 squares, 4⅞" x 4⅞". Cut once diagonally to yield 14 half-square triangles. (You will use 13.)

From the pale yellow floral, cut:
- 2 strips, 24" x 42", crosscut *each* strip into:
  - 1 square, 24" x 24". Cut twice diagonally to yield 4 side triangles (8 total).
  - 1 square, 12½" x 12½". Cut once diagonally to yield 2 corner triangles (4 total).
- 17 strips, 4½" x 42"; crosscut into:
  - 26 rectangles, 4½" x 12½"
  - 26 rectangles, 4½" x 8½"
  - 13 squares, 4½" x 4½"
- 1 strip, 4⅞" x 42"; crosscut into 7 squares, 4⅞" x 4⅞"

From the orange print, cut:
- 2 strips, 4½" x 42"; crosscut into 13 squares, 4½" x 4½"
- 1 strip, 4⅞" x 42"; crosscut into 7 squares, 4⅞" x 4⅞"

From the purple print, cut:
- 2 strips, 4½" x 42"; crosscut into 13 squares, 4½" x 4½"
- 1 strip, 4⅞" x 42"; crosscut into 7 squares, 4⅞" x 4⅞". Cut once diagonally to yield 14 half-square triangles. (You will use 13.)

From the green print, cut:
- 2 strips, 8⅞" x 42"; crosscut into 7 squares, 8⅞" x 8⅞". Cut once diagonally to yield 14 half-square triangles. (You will use 13.)
- 1 strip, 4⅞" x 42"; crosscut into 7 squares, 4⅞" x 4⅞"

From the pink print for binding, cut:
- 7 strips, 2¼" x 42"

Making the Bouquet Blocks

1. Draw a diagonal line on the wrong side of each 4½" pink and blue square. With right sides together, place a marked pink square at one end of a 4½" x 8½" pale yellow rectangle as shown. Sew on the drawn line. Trim ¼" from the stitched line and press the seam allowance toward the corner. Place a marked blue square at the opposite end of each rectangle. Be sure the diagonal line is oriented in the opposite direction of the first square. Sew, trim, and press as before.

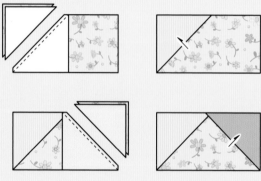

Make 13.

2. Repeat step 1 using the 4½" orange and purple squares, and the 4½" x 8½" pale yellow rectangles.

Make 13.

3. Draw a diagonal line on the wrong side of each 4⅞" pink square. Place each square right sides together with a 4⅞" orange square. Sew ¼" from each side of the drawn line. Cut the squares apart on the line and press the seam allowances toward the orange triangles. You will make 14 triangle squares but you will use only 13.

Make 14.

4. Sew a blue triangle to the pink side of each triangle square from step 3 as shown. Press the seam allowance toward the blue triangle. Sew a purple triangle to the orange side as shown. Press the seam allowance toward the purple triangle.

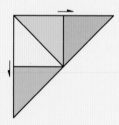

Make 13.

5. Sew an 8⅞" green triangle to each unit from step 4 as shown. Place the pieced unit on top so you can see the intersection point when you sew. Press the seam allowance toward the green triangle.

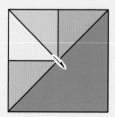

Make 13.

6. Lay out the units from step 5, the pieced rectangles from steps 1 and 2, and 13 pale yellow 4½" squares as shown. Sew the units into vertical rows, pressing the seam allowances as shown. Sew the rows together, and press the seam allowance toward the pale yellow square.

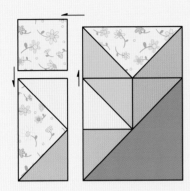

7. Draw a diagonal line on the wrong side of each 4⅞" pale yellow square. Place each square right sides together with a 4⅞" green square. Sew ¼" from each side of the drawn line. Cut the squares apart on the line and press the seam allowances toward the green triangles. You will make 14 triangle squares but you will use only 13.

Make 14.

8. Sew a 4½" x 12½" pale yellow rectangle to the right edge of each unit from step 6 as shown. Then sew a triangle square from step 7 to a 4½" x 12½" pale yellow rectangle as shown. Press the seam allowances toward the rectangle. Sew these strips to the bottom of each unit as shown. Press the seam allowances toward the rectangle strips. Make 13 Bouquet blocks.

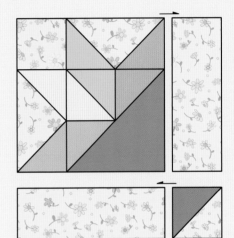

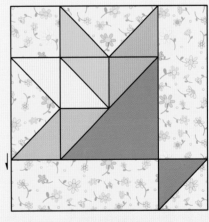

Bouquet block.
Make 13.

Assembling the Quilt Top

1. Lay out the pieced blocks, side triangles, and corner triangles as shown in the assembly diagram below. Sew the blocks and side triangles into diagonal rows and press the seam allowances as shown. Sew the rows together and press the seams in either direction. Sew a corner triangle to each corner of the quilt top and press the seams toward the corners.

2. Trim the edges of the quilt top, leaving a ¼" seam allowance beyond the block points. Square up the four corners.

Finishing the Quilt

Refer to "Preparing to Quilt" on page 119, "Quilting Techniques" on page 120, and "Finishing Techniques" on page 121 for more detailed instructions, if needed.

1. Piece the quilt backing so that it is 4" to 6" longer and wider than the quilt top. Mark the quilt top if necessary. Layer the quilt top with batting and backing, and baste the layers together.

2. Hand or machine quilt as desired.

3. Trim the batting and backing even with the edges of the quilt top. Add a hanging sleeve if desired. Using the seven 2¼"-wide pink strips, prepare the binding and sew it to the quilt. Make a label and attach it to your quilt.

LOG CABIN POLKA

From *Follow the Dots . . . to Dazzling Quilts* by Jayme Crow and Joan Segna.
Pieced by Jayme Crow and machine quilted by Sandy Sims.

Finished Quilt Size: 56" x 74½"
Finished Block Size: 18½" x 18½"

This scrappy variation of a Log Cabin quilt hearkens back to the early days
of the United States, when scraps of fabric and usable pieces of clothing were recycled
into warm bed quilts. Bright colors were especially treasured because
they added a touch of sparkle and cheer. So, turn on the polka music,
dig into your scrap bag, and create a one-of-a-kind treasure!

Materials

Yardage is based on 42"-wide fabric.

- 168 pieces of fabric, 10" x 13", for blocks*
- ⅛ yard of black print for block centers
- ⅝ yard of fabric for binding
- 3½ yards of fabric for backing
- 62" x 80" piece of batting
- 12 buttons for embellishing (optional)

**See "Cutting" below. You can use scraps for many of
the pieces.*

Cutting

All measurements include ¼" seam allowances. Instructions are for cutting strips across the fabric width.

To make a totally scrappy quilt, cut just one block at a time. Use 14 different fabrics for each block and plan each block before cutting. Each 18½" square block is made up of four quadrants, referred to as units A, B, C, and D. Choose fabrics for each piece, and as you cut, label the pieces with the unit letter and the piece number.

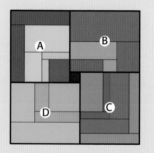

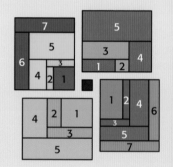

For One Block

From fabric #1, cut:
- 1 rectangle, 3½" x 3¾" (A-1)

From fabric #2, cut:
- 1 rectangle, 1½" x 3¾" (A-2)
- 1 rectangle, 1½" x 4½" (A-3)

From fabric #3, cut:
- 1 rectangle, 3" x 4¾" (A-4)
- 1 rectangle, 4¼" x 7" (A-5)

From fabric #4, cut:
- 1 rectangle, 2½" x 8½" (A-6)
- 1 rectangle, 2½" x 9" (A-7)

From fabric #5, cut:
- 1 rectangle, 2¼" x 5¼" (B-1)

From fabric #6, cut:
- 1 rectangle, 2¼" x 2½" (B-2)
- 1 rectangle, 3" x 7¼" (B-3)

From fabric #7, cut:
- 1 rectangle, 3¾" x 4¾" (B-4)
- 1 rectangle, 4¾" x 10½" (B-5)

From fabric #8, cut:
- 1 rectangle, 3¾" x 6" (C-1)

From fabric #9, cut:
- 1 rectangle, 1½" x 6" (C-2)
- 1 rectangle, 1½" x 4¾" (C-3)

From fabric #10, cut:
- 1 rectangle, 3¼" x 7" (C-4)
- 1 rectangle, 2½" x 7½" (C-5)

From fabric #11, cut:
- 2 rectangles, 2" x 9" (C-6 and C-7)

From fabric #12, cut:
- 1 rectangle, 4½" x 5" (D-1)

From fabric #13, cut:
- 1 rectangle, 2½" x 4½" (D-2)
- 1 rectangle, 2" x 7" (D-3)

From fabric #14, cut:
- 1 rectangle, 4" x 6" (D-4)
- 1 rectangle, 3½" x 10½" (D-5)

From the black print, cut:
- 1 square, 2" x 2" (center square)

For the Binding

From the binding fabric, cut:
- 7 strips, 2¼" x 42"

Making the Log Cabin Blocks

Each quadrant or unit of the block is pieced similar to a half Log Cabin block. The rectangles are sewn onto two alternating sides of the first piece in each unit. Refer to the illustrations and assemble the block units as directed below.

NOTE: *Press after each seam is stitched, and press all seams away from the first piece in the unit.*

Unit A

1. Sew piece A-2 to the left edge of A-1.
2. Sew piece A-3 to the top edge of the unit just sewn.
3. Sew piece A-4 to the left edge of the unit.
4. Sew piece A-5 to the top edge of the unit.
5. Sew piece A-6 to the left edge of the unit.
6. Sew piece A-7 to the top edge of the unit.

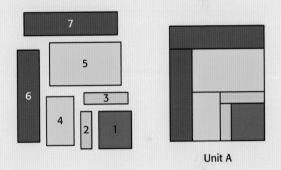
Unit A

Unit B

1. Sew piece B-2 to the right edge of B-1.
2. Sew piece B-3 to the top edge of the unit just sewn.
3. Sew piece B-4 to the right edge of the unit.
4. Sew piece B-5 to the top edge of the unit.

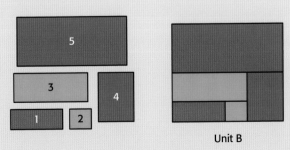
Unit B

Unit C

1. Sew piece C-2 to the right edge of C-1.

2. Sew piece C-3 to the bottom edge of the unit just sewn.

3. Sew piece C-4 to the right edge of the unit.

4. Sew piece C-5 to the bottom edge of the unit.

5. Sew piece C-6 to the right edge of the unit.

6. Sew piece C-7 to the bottom edge of the unit.

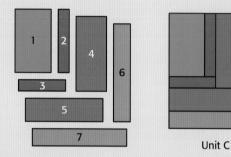

Unit C

Unit D

1. Sew piece D-2 to the left edge of D-1.

2. Sew piece D-3 to the bottom edge of the unit just sewn.

3. Sew piece D-4 to the left edge of the unit.

4. Sew piece D-5 to the bottom edge of the unit.

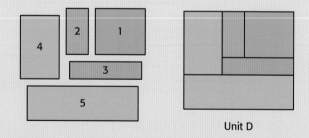

Unit D

Joining the Units

1. To assemble the block units, you will sew around the 2" black-print center square counterclockwise, using a partial seam at the first join. With right sides together, line up the 2" square with the bottom of unit A as shown.

Begin in the middle of the 2" square and stitch to the bottom edge of unit A. Press away from the center square.

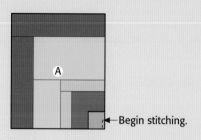

2. Sew unit D to the bottom edge of unit A and the 2" square; press.

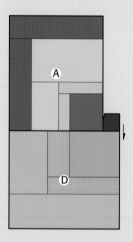

3. Sew unit C to the right edge of unit D and the 2" square; press.

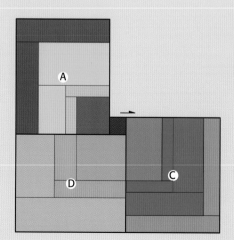

4. Before sewing unit B to the top edge of unit C and the 2" square, make sure the loose piece of unit A is out of the way. Sew unit B, and press away from the center square.

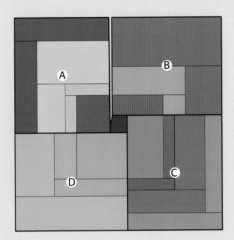

5. Sew the seam between unit A, the 2" square, and unit B, beginning in the middle of the 2" square. Press away from the center square. The block is complete, and it should measure 19" x 19".

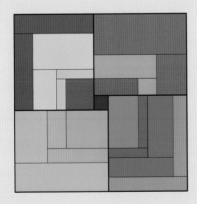

6. Repeat "Cutting" and "Making the Log Cabin Blocks" to make the remaining 11 blocks.

Assembling the Quilt Top

1. Arrange the blocks in four rows of three blocks each as shown.

2. Sew the blocks into rows. Press the seams in opposite directions from row to row.

3. Sew the rows together. Press the seams in one direction.

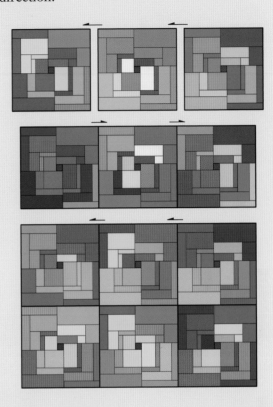

Finishing the Quilt

Refer to "Preparing to Quilt" on page 119, "Quilting Techniques" on page 120, and "Finishing Techniques" on page 121 for more detailed instructions, if needed.

1. Piece the quilt backing so that it is 4" to 6" longer and wider than the quilt top. Mark the quilt top if necessary. Layer the quilt top with batting and backing, and baste the layers together.

2. Hand or machine quilt as desired.

3. Trim the batting and backing even with the edges of the quilt top. Add a hanging sleeve if desired. Using the 2¼"-wide binding strips, prepare the binding and sew it to the quilt. Make a label and attach it to your quilt.

4. Add a button to the center of each block if desired.

HOLIDAY TOPPER

From *Crazy Eights* by Mary Sue Suit. Quilt pieced by Mary Sue Suit and quilted by Judy Woodworth.

Finished Quilt Size: 68½" x 80½"
Finished Block Size: 6½" x 16"

Mary Sue calls this a "topper" quilt because when placed on top of a plain bedspread, it is just the right size to top off a double bed. It is also large enough to "top off" anyone lounging in a recliner. Its design is fat-quarter friendly, so expansion is easy. Choose varied color values in order to see the diamonds within rectangles within diamonds.

Materials

Yardage is based on 42"-wide fabric.

- 2½ yards of fabric for outer border and binding
- 1½ yards of multicolored batik for background
- 1 fat quarter *each* of 4 medium golds for blocks and inner border
- 1 fat quarter *each* of 3 dark reds for blocks and inner border
- 1 fat quarter *each* of 3 dark greens for blocks and inner border
- 1 fat quarter *each* of 2 medium reds for blocks and inner border
- 1 fat quarter *each* of 2 medium greens for blocks and inner border
- 1 fat quarter *each* of 2 dark golds for blocks and inner border
- 4 yards of fabric for backing
- 72" x 84" piece of batting
- Mary Sue's Triangle Ruler®* (optional)

*This quilt was made using Mary Sue's Triangle Ruler (available from Martingale & Company). It can also be made using the template pattern on page 87. The template is not a duplicate of the ruler but provides the shape and measurements needed to cut the pieces. The ruler is shown in the project illustrations.

Cutting

All measurements include ¼" seam allowances. Instructions are for cutting strips across the fabric width.

The following list is the initial set of cutting instructions. From the pieces on this list, additional cuts will be made using several cutting methods. These methods are described after the cutting list.

From *each* of the dark red fat quarters, cut:
- 1 rectangle, 8" x 18"

From 2 of the dark red fat quarters, cut:
- 1 strip, 5¼" x 21"

From *each* of the medium red fat quarters, cut:
- 1 strip, 5¼" x 21"

From 1 of the medium red fat quarters, cut:
- 4 rectangles, 4½" x 9"

From the *second* medium red fat quarter, cut:
- 2 rectangles, 4½" x 9"

From *each* of the dark green fat quarters, cut:
- 1 rectangle, 8" x 18"

From 2 of the dark green fat quarters, cut:
- 1 strip, 5¼" x 21"

From *each* of the medium green fat quarters, cut:
- 1 strip, 5¼" x 21"

From 1 of the medium green fat quarters, cut:
- 4 rectangles, 4½" x 9"

From the *second* medium green fat quarter, cut:
- 2 rectangles, 4½" x 9"

From *each* of the medium gold fat quarters, cut:
- 1 rectangle, 8" x 18"

From 2 of the medium gold fat quarters, cut:
- 1 strip, 5¼" x 21"

From *each* of the dark gold fat quarters, cut:
- 4 rectangles, 4½" x 9"

From 2 of the dark gold fat quarters, cut:
- 1 strip, 5¼" x 21"

From the multicolored batik, cut:
- 1 strip, 9" x 21"
- 2 strips, 8½" x 42"
- 3 strips, 3¾" x 42"
- 2 rectangles, 8" x 18"
- 2 rectangles, 4½" x 9"

From the outer border and binding fabric, cut:
- 8 strips, 6½" x 42"
- 8 strips, 2¼" x 42"

Background Triangles

You need two background triangles for each basic pieced triangle unit, so keep the triangles in pairs to help your piecing session go smoothly.

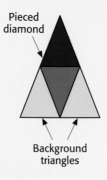

Pieced diamond

Background triangles

1. Fold a 5¼" x 21" strip in half crosswise. Place the triangle ruler on the strip just inside the selvages, with the 5¼" line aligned with the bottom edge of the strip. Cut along both edges.

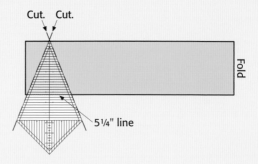

Cut. Cut.

Fold

5¼" line

2. Rotate the ruler so that the 5¼" line is aligned with the top edge of the strip and the side of the ruler is aligned with the previous cut. Then cut along the right edge of the ruler.

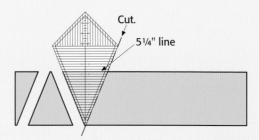

Cut.

5¼" line

3. Continue in this manner to cut the number of triangles required from the remainder of the strip. Quantity information will be provided in the block instructions.

Large 45° Triangles

These triangles are the same size as the basic pieced triangle unit. They are cut the same as the background triangles but from a 9"-wide strip. Mary Sue's Triangle Ruler is not quite large enough to cut across the 9" strip, so some sliding is necessary.

1. Fold the 9" x 21" strip in half crosswise. Place the triangle ruler on the strip with the 45° tip facing downward and the centerline on the selvages. Align the 2" line with the top edge of the strip. Beginning at the bottom of the ruler, cut along the right side of the ruler as far as you can, and then slide the ruler up to make the full cut, keeping the edge of the ruler aligned with the edge you just cut. Discard the piece cut from the end of the strip or set it aside for use in another project.

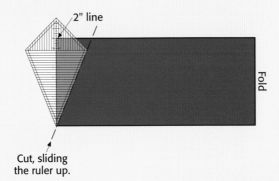

Cut, sliding
the ruler up.

2. Rotate the ruler so that the 2" line of the ruler is aligned with the bottom edge of the strip. Cut along the right edge of the ruler, beginning the cut halfway down the ruler and cutting up. Slide the ruler down to finish the cut in the same manner as before.

Cut, starting halfway down the ruler
and cutting up and then sliding the ruler
down to complete the cut.

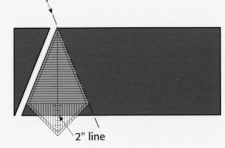

2" line

3. Continue in this manner to cut the number of triangles required from the remainder of the strip. Quantity information will be provided in the block instructions.

90° Triangles

These triangles are used on the sides of 45° triangles to give you a straight edge to work with. They are cut in pairs from two rectangles that have been layered with the same sides together. This ensures that you have a right and a left piece. Each pair of rectangles will yield two sets of 90° triangles.

90° triangles

1. Layer the 4½" x 9" rectangles right sides together. At the top of the rectangles, measure 4¼" from the left edge and make a mark as shown. At the bottom of the rectangles, measure ¼" from the left edge and make a mark as shown.

4¼"

¼"

2. Place a straight-edged rotary ruler on the rectangles to connect the marks. Cut to yield two sets.

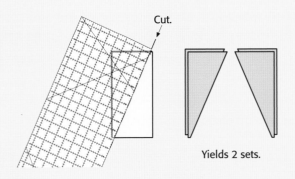

Cut.

Yields 2 sets.

Making the Basic Pieced Triangle Blocks

This block consists of two pieced diamonds, two pairs of background triangles, and four 90° triangles. You will need to make 10 blocks.

1. To make the pieced diamonds, layer each dark red 5¼" x 21" strip with a medium red 5¼" x 21" strip, right sides together. Sew ¼" from the top and bottom edges of each pair of strips.

2. Place the triangle ruler on a sewn strip, with the 4¾" line aligned with the seam at the bottom of the strip. The tip of the ruler will be at the seam line across the top of the strip. Cut along both sides of the ruler to cut one pieced diamond.

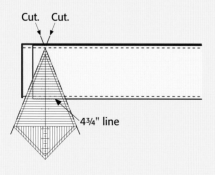

Cut. Cut.

4¾" line

3. Rotate the ruler so that the 4¾" line is aligned with the seam line at the top of the strip. Cut along the right side of the ruler. Continue rotating the ruler in this manner to cut eight pieced diamonds from one pair of fabrics and six pieced diamonds from the other pair. Press the seams open to reveal the pieced diamonds. You should be able to cut eight pieced diamonds from a 5¼" x 21" strip pair.

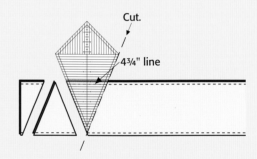

Cut.

4¾" line

4. Repeat steps 1–3 with one dark green and one medium green 5¼" x 21" strip to cut six pieced diamonds.

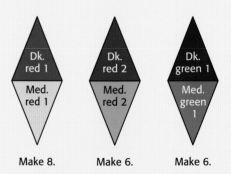

Dk. red 1 / Med. red 1 — Make 8.

Dk. red 2 / Med. red 2 — Make 6.

Dk. green 1 / Med. green 1 — Make 6.

5. Refer to "Background Triangles" on page 78 to cut background triangles from the remaining medium green, dark green, medium gold, and dark gold 5¼" x 21" strips. Cut four sets (eight triangles total) from each green strip. Cut four sets (eight triangles total) each from one dark gold and one medium gold strip. Cut two sets (four triangles total) from the remaining dark gold and medium gold strips. You should have a total of 40 background triangles.

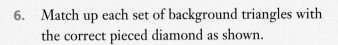

6. Match up each set of background triangles with the correct pieced diamond as shown.

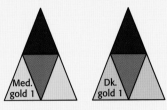

Med. gold 1   Dk. gold 1

Make 3 each.

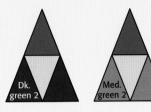

Dk. green 2   Med. green 2

Make 4 each.

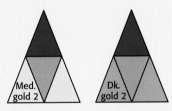

Med. gold 2   Dk. gold 2

Make 3 each.

7. Position a background triangle on the upper-right edge of each pieced diamond, right sides together as shown. Match the top corner of the triangle to the tip of the diamond. The tip of the triangle will extend below the seam of the pieced diamond. Stitch ¼" from the edge. Press the seam toward the background triangle.

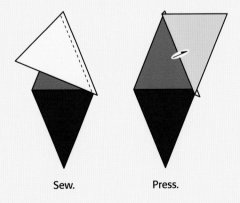

Sew.   Press.

8. Repeat to add the other background triangle to the upper-left edge of each pieced diamond. Press the seam toward the diamond.

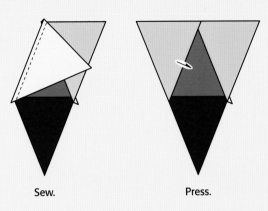

Sew.   Press.

9. To trim, place a pieced triangle unit on the cutting surface, with the background triangles at the bottom as shown. Position the triangle ruler on the unit, with the 4¾" line on the horizontal seam line of the pieced diamond and the 2¼" line on the 90° corner of the ruler at the lower tip of the pieced diamond as shown. The ¼" side seam line on the ruler should cross the seam intersections of the pieced diamond and background triangles. Trim any excess. You will need to slide the ruler down along the trimmed upper side edges to trim the lower side edges.

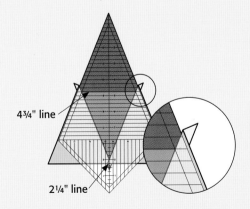

4¾" line

2¼" line

NOTE: *These measurements depend on a full ¼" seam allowance. If your triangle is a bit large, check your seams and adjust as necessary.*

10. Turn the pieced triangle unit so that the background triangles are at the top as shown. Position the triangle ruler on the unit, with the crossbar line on the trimmed left side edge and the ¼" seam allowance aligned across the tip of the pieced diamond. Cut across the background triangles to complete the trimming process.

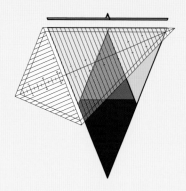

11. Referring to "90° Triangles" on page 79, cut two 90° triangles from each 4½" x 9" fat-quarter and multicolored batik rectangle. Set the multicolored batik 90° triangles aside for later use.

12. Stitch the fat-quarter 90° triangles to the sides of the basic pieced triangle units as shown to make the half-block combinations.

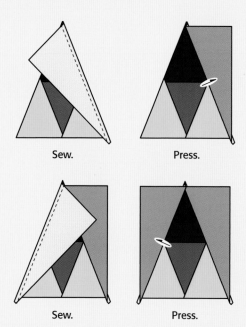

Sew. Press.

Sew. Press.

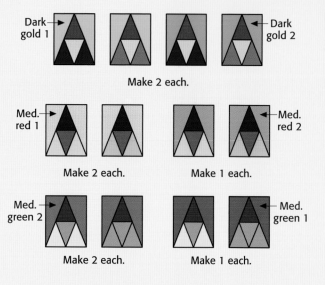

Dark gold 1 →   ← Dark gold 2

Make 2 each.

Med. red 1 →   ← Med. red 2

Make 2 each.   Make 1 each.

Med. green 2 →   ← Med. green 1

Make 2 each.   Make 1 each.

13. Sew the half blocks from step 12 together as shown. Trim the blocks to 7" x 16½". You should have a total of 10 Basic Pieced Triangle blocks.

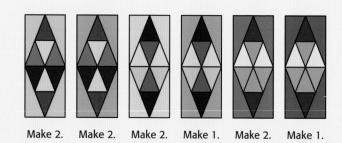

Make 2. Make 2. Make 2. Make 1. Make 2. Make 1.

Making the Remaining Blocks

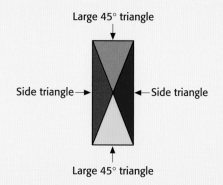

Large 45° triangle

Side triangle →   ← Side triangle

Large 45° triangle

1. On each end of each fat-quarter 8" x 18" rectangle, measure ¼" in from both long edges and

make a mark as shown. Using your rotary cutter and a long ruler, connect the marks diagonally and cut each rectangle in half. Without moving the pieces, cut each rectangle across the opposite diagonal.

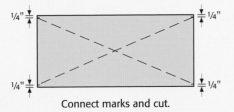

Connect marks and cut.

2. Referring to "Large 45° Triangles" on page 78, use the 9" x 21" strip of multicolored batik to cut four 45° triangles. Match up these triangles and the pieces from step 1 to make one of each of the blocks shown below, using the multicolored batik 45° triangles where indicated. You will have pieces left over to use later in step 8.

Make 1 of each.

3. With right sides together, place a side triangle from step 1 on the right edge of a 45° triangle. Extend the point of the 45° triangle above the point of the side triangle so that the first stitch will go through both pieces of fabric; stitch. Press the seams toward the side triangle. Repeat to make 14 half blocks.

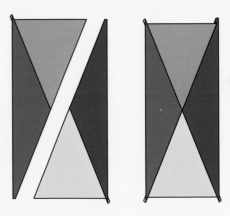

Sew.

4. Sew the two halves together. The seams should cross at the ¼" mark so that the tips of the large triangles will match and be sharp.

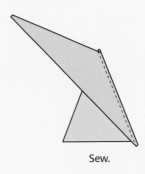

5. Trim the seven blocks to 7" x 16½". To trim each block evenly, lay it horizontally on the cutting surface. Place a long rotary-cutting ruler on the block, with the 8¼" vertical line positioned where the tips of the 45° triangles meet and the

¼" horizontal line positioned at the base point of the 45° triangle as shown. Trim along the right edge and top of the block.

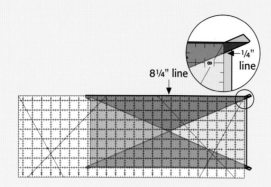

6. Rotate the block 180°. Align the left edge of the block with the 16½" vertical line on the ruler, the tips of the 45° triangles with the 8¼" vertical line, and the base point of the 45° triangle with the ¼" horizontal line as shown. Trim along the right edge and top of the block.

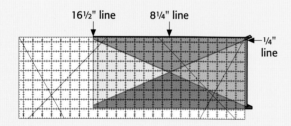

7. Mark ¼" from opposite ends of the two 8" x 18" multicolored batik rectangles as shown. Cut the rectangles in half diagonally from mark to mark.

8. Sew the half rectangles from step 7 and the appropriate remaining side and 45° triangles

together to make one of each of the blocks shown. Trim the blocks as you did in steps 5 and 6 to 7" x 16½".

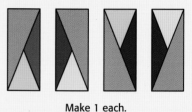

Make 1 each.

9. Fold the remaining gold side triangles in half; lightly crease them to mark the centers. Open up the triangles. Place the 8½" line of your long ruler on the center mark of one triangle; cut off the tip that extends beyond the ruler. Repeat on the opposite side of the triangle. Trim the remaining triangle in the same manner.

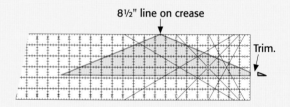

10. Lay one of the multicolored batik 90° triangles that you set aside earlier on one short side of each trimmed triangle, right sides together; stitch. Repeat on the opposite short side. Make two.

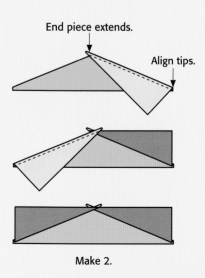

Make 2.

11. Trim the blocks to 3¾" x 16½". To trim the block evenly, place the block horizontally on the cutting surface. Lay your long ruler on the block, with the ruler 8¼" vertical line through the center of the triangle and the ¼" horizontal line of the ruler at the tip of the triangle. Trim along the right and top edges. Repeat on the opposite end of the blocks.

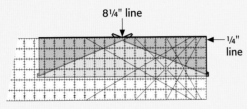

Trim top and side edges.

12. Place the 3¾" horizontal line of the ruler along the top edge of the block. Trim the bottom edge. These are the blocks for the ends of row 3.

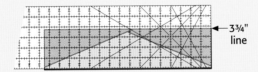

Trim bottom edge.

13. Fold each multicolored batik 8½" x 42" strip in half crosswise. For each strip, mark 6¾" from the bottom edge. Lay your triangle ruler on the strip, with the tip on the mark as shown and the 2½" line on the 90° corner of the ruler at the top edge. Cut along the right edge of the ruler to create one set of end pieces. Mark 6¾" from the top of the angled cut. Lay your triangle ruler on the strip, with the left edge at the mark. Cut along the left edge of the ruler to make two trapezoids.

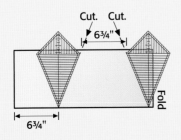

Assembling the Quilt-Top Center

Arrange the blocks, end pieces, and trapezoids as shown to make the five rows. Stitch the pieces in each row together. Sew rows 1 and 2 together and rows 4 and 5 together. Sew the three multicolored batik 3¾"-wide strips end to end. From this long strip, cut four pieces, 24½" long. Stitch one of these multicolored batik 24½"-long strips to each end of the joined rows. Sew the row 1-2 unit to row 3; press. Sew the row 4-5 unit to the other side of row 3; press.

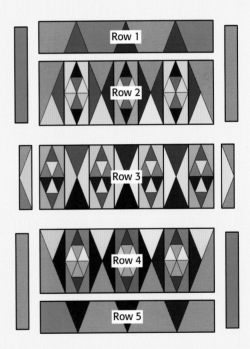

Adding the Borders

1. From the remainder of the fat quarters, cut 2½"-wide strips. You may cut the strips any length to achieve the desired effect. Randomly sew the strips together end to end.

2. From one of the 6½"-wide outer-border strips, cut eight corner triangles, positioning the triangle ruler on the strip with the 6½" line of the ruler at the top or bottom of the strip alternately. Stitch the corner triangles together in pairs. Make four.

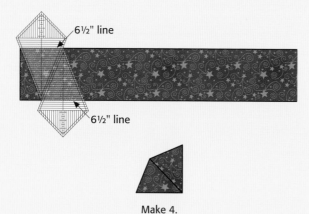

Make 4.

3. Referring to "Borders with Corner Squares" on page 118, attach the 2½"-wide pieced inner border, the 6½"-wide outer border, and the four corner triangle pairs to the quilt top.

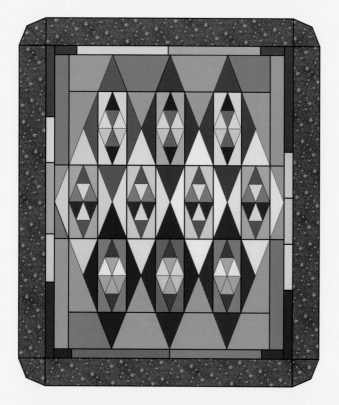

Finishing the Quilt

Refer to "Preparing to Quilt" on page 119, "Quilting Techniques" on page 120, and "Finishing Techniques" on page 121 for more detailed instructions, if needed.

1. Piece the quilt backing so that it is 4" to 6" longer and wider than the quilt top. Mark the quilt top if necessary. Layer the quilt top with batting and backing, and baste the layers together.

2. Hand or machine quilt as desired.

3. Trim the batting and backing even with the edges of the quilt top. Add a hanging sleeve if desired. Using the 2¼"-wide binding strips, prepare the binding and sew it to the quilt. Make a label and attach it to your quilt.

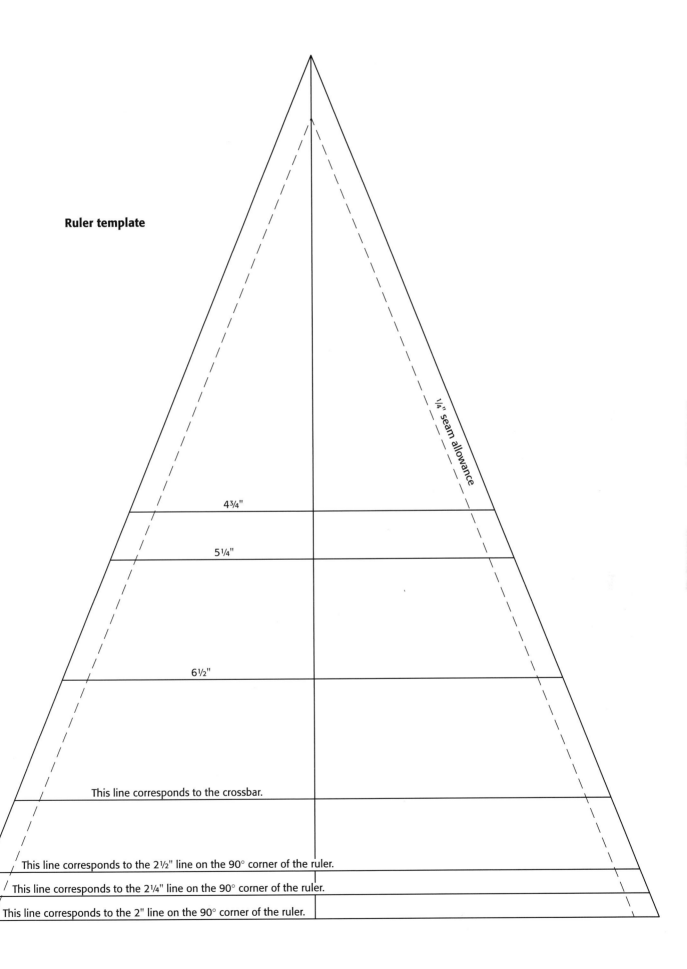

Ruler template

¼" seam allowance

4¾"

5¼"

6½"

This line corresponds to the crossbar.

This line corresponds to the 2½" line on the 90° corner of the ruler.

This line corresponds to the 2¼" line on the 90° corner of the ruler.

This line corresponds to the 2" line on the 90° corner of the ruler.

SCOTCH GRANNY QUILT

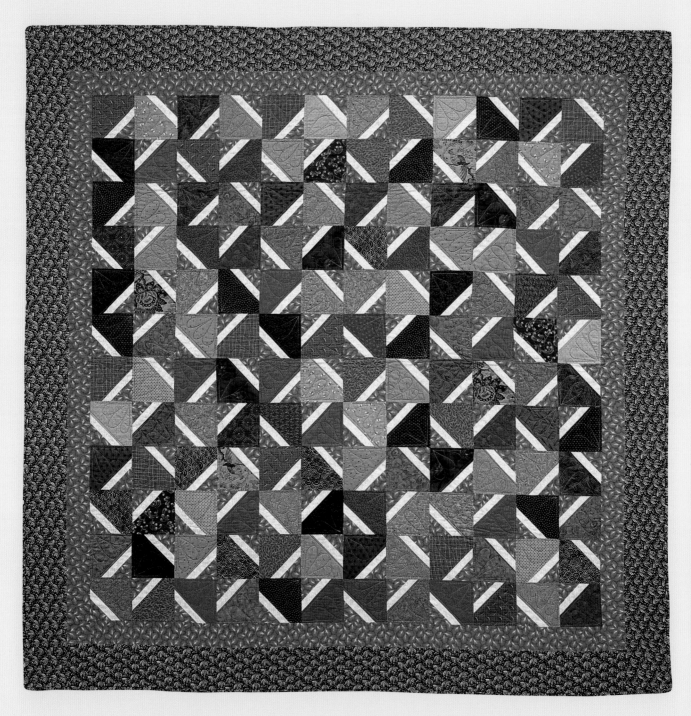

From *Joined at the Heart* by Anne Moscicki and Linda Wyckoff-Hickey.
Quilt made by Anne Moscicki and Linda Wyckoff-Hickey, and quilted by Celeste Marshall.

Finished Quilt Size: 83½" x 83½"
Finished Block Size: 5½" x 5½"

Chances are good that every quiltmaker has heard parents or grandparents tell of days when there wasn't a scrap to waste. This quilt design honors that hard-learned lesson—as valuable today as it was necessary then—by using two simple "flips" on each block to stretch one project into two. These quilt directions will yield additional blocks that you can use to make "Scotch Granny Throw" on page 92.

Materials

Yardage is based on 42"-wide fabric.

- 2½ yards of tan print for blocks
- 2¼ yards of dark blue print for outer border and binding
- 2⅛ yards of red print for blocks and inner border
- ¼ yard *each* of 24 assorted medium and dark fabrics for blocks*
- 7½ yards of fabric for backing
- 89" x 89" piece of batting

* You may substitute 144 squares, 6" x 6", of assorted scraps.

Cutting

All measurements include ¼" seam allowances. Instructions are for cutting strips across the fabric width.

From the tan print, cut:
- 18 strips, 4½" x 42"; crosscut into 144 squares, 4½" x 4½"

From *each* of the medium and dark fabrics, cut:
- 1 strip, 6" x 42"; crosscut into 6 squares, 6" x 6" (144 total)*

From the red print, cut:
- 12 strips, 3¼" x 42"; crosscut into 144 squares, 3¼" x 3¼"
- 7 strips, 3½" x 42"

From the dark blue print, cut:
- 8 strips, 6" x 42"
- 9 strips, 2½" x 42"

* You won't need to cut these pieces if you are using precut scraps.

Making the Double Back-Flips Blocks

You will use one medium or dark square, one tan print square, and one red print square to complete the Double Back-Flips block shown below. This is the block you will use to construct "Scotch Granny Quilt." The method used to make each block yields two additional blocks that can be used to piece "Scotch Granny Throw," shown on page 92.

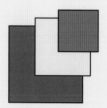

1. Place one tan print square over the upper-right corner of a medium or dark square, right sides together and raw edges aligned. Mark the smaller square once diagonally from corner to corner, and then move the ruler ½" toward the upper-right corner of the square and mark a second line parallel to the first as shown. Sew on both marked lines. Cut the squares halfway between the two stitching lines. Make 144.

Make 144.

2. Fold out the corners on each unit from step 1; press. Set aside the small triangle squares to use for "Scotch Granny Throw" or another project.

3. Repeat step 1 using a red print square and the unit from step 2. Make 144.

Make 144.

4. Fold the corners out on each unit from step 3; press. Set aside the small triangle squares to use for "Scotch Granny Throw" or another project. Trim each Double Back-Flips block to 6" x 6" as necessary.

Assembling the Quilt Top

1. Referring to the assembly diagram below and the quilt photo on page 88, lay out the blocks in 12 horizontal rows of 12 blocks each, rotating them as shown and balancing the placement of color as you go.

2. Sew the blocks together into rows; press. Sew the rows together, interlocking the seam allowances; press.

3. Referring to "Borders with Butted Corners" on page 117, attach the 3½"-wide red inner border and the 6"-wide dark blue outer border to the quilt top.

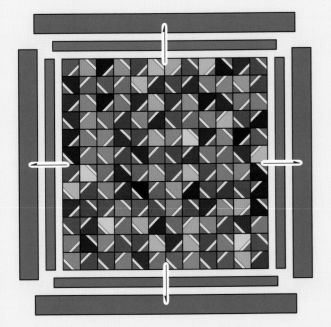

Finishing the Quilt

Refer to "Preparing to Quilt" on page 119, "Quilting Techniques" on page 120, and "Finishing Techniques" on page 121 for more detailed instructions, if needed.

1. Piece the quilt backing so that it is 4" to 6" longer and wider than the quilt top. Mark the quilt top if necessary. Layer the quilt top with batting and backing, and baste the layers together.

2. Hand or machine quilt as desired.

3. Trim the batting and backing even with the edges of the quilt top. Add a hanging sleeve if desired. Using the 2½"-wide binding strips, prepare the binding and sew it to the quilt. Make a label and attach it to your quilt.

From *Joined at the Heart* by Anne Moscicki and Linda Wyckoff-Hickey.
Quilt made by Anne Moscicki and Linda Wyckoff-Hickey, and quilted by Celeste Marshall.

Finished Quilt Size: 45½" x 45½"
Finished Block Size: 6" x 6"

Waste not, want not! What more could you wish for than two quilts for the fabric of one?
Now the leftover blocks you made during construction of "Scotch Granny Quilt,"
shown on page 88, are ready to sparkle and shine on their own in this playful throw.
If you just want to make the throw "from scratch," yardage, a cutting list,
and instructions appear on page 95.

Materials

Yardage is based on 42"-wide fabric.

- ⅝ yard of fabric for outer border
- ⅝ yard of fabric for binding
- 3⅛ yards of fabric for backing
- 54" x 54" piece of batting

Cutting

All measurements include ¼" seam allowances. Instructions are for cutting strips across the fabric width.

From the outer-border fabric, cut:
- 5 strips, 3" x 42"

From the binding fabric, cut:
- 6 strips, 2½" x 42"

Making the Pinwheel Blocks

You will use the larger leftover triangle squares from "Scotch Granny Quilt" to make these blocks. Before you begin, trim the units to 3½" as necessary.

Arrange four triangle squares into two rows of two blocks each as shown, matching colors whenever possible. Part of the scrappy, quirky charm of this quilt is that some of the blocks won't match perfectly, so don't worry if you're mixing reds and blues in one pinwheel. Make 36 Pinwheel blocks, squaring each to 6½" as necessary.

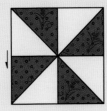

Make 36.

Assembling the Quilt-Top Center

Referring to the quilt photo on page 92 and the assembly diagram below, lay out the Pinwheel blocks in six horizontal rows of six blocks each as shown, balancing the placement of color as you go. Sew the blocks together into rows; press. Sew the rows together, interlocking the seam allowances; press.

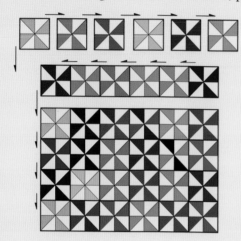

Adding the Borders

Use the smaller leftover triangle squares from "Scotch Granny Quilt" to make these borders. Before you begin, trim the units to 2½" as necessary.

1. Arrange and sew the triangle squares as shown to make the pieced inner borders. Each side border strip is made with 18 triangle squares. Make two; press. The longer top and bottom border strips are each made with 20 triangle squares. Make two; press.

Make 2.

Make 2.

2. Sew the shorter pieced inner-border strips to the sides of the quilt top as shown, pinning

carefully to match the seams. Press the seams toward the border strips. Sew the longer pieced strips to the top and bottom of the quilt top; press. Refer to "Easing" on page 113 as necessary.

3. Referring to "Borders with Butted Corners" on page 117, attach the 3"-wide outer border to the quilt top.

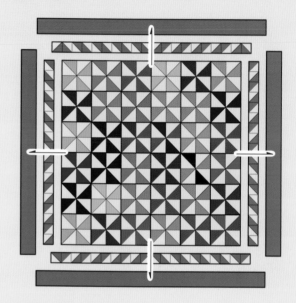

Finishing the Quilt

Refer to "Preparing to Quilt" on page 119, "Quilting Techniques" on page 120, and "Finishing Techniques" on page 121 for more detailed instructions, if needed.

1. Piece the quilt backing so that it is 4" to 6" longer and wider than the quilt top. Mark the quilt top if necessary. Layer the quilt top with batting and backing, and baste the layers together.

2. Hand or machine quilt as desired.

3. Trim the batting and backing even with the edges of the quilt top. Add a hanging sleeve if desired. Using the 2½"-wide binding strips, prepare the binding and sew it to the quilt. Make a label and attach it to your quilt.

MAKING SCOTCH GRANNY THROW FROM SCRATCH

IF YOU DON'T have leftover blocks from making "Scotch Granny Quilt" on page 88, follow these directions to make "Scotch Granny Throw" from scratch.

Materials

Yardage is based on 42"-wide fabric. Yardages for the outer border, binding, backing, and batting are identical to those listed on page 93 for "Scotch Granny Throw." In addition, you will need:

- 1½ yards of tan print for Pinwheel blocks and inner border
- ⅜ yard of red print for inner border
- ¼ yard *each* of 12 assorted medium and dark fabrics for Pinwheel blocks*

* You may substitute 72 squares, 4⅜" x 4⅜", of assorted scraps.

Cutting

All measurements include ¼" seam allowances. Instructions are for cutting strips across the fabric width.

NOTE: *Follow the cutting instructions for the outer border and binding listed on page 93 for "Scotch Granny Throw." In addition, you will need:*

From the tan print, cut:
- 9 strips, 4⅜" x 42"; crosscut into 72 squares, 4⅜" x 4⅜"
- 3 strips, 2⅞" x 42"; crosscut into 38 squares, 2⅞" x 2⅞"

From *each* of the medium and dark fabrics, cut:
- 1 strip, 4⅜" x 42"; crosscut into 6 squares, 4⅜" x 4⅜" (72 total)*

From the red print, cut:
- 3 strips, 2⅞" x 42"; crosscut into 38 squares, 2⅞" x 2⅞"

*You won't need to cut these pieces if you are using precut scraps.

Making the Triangle Squares

1. Layer one tan print 4⅜" square with one medium or dark 4⅜" square, right sides together and raw edges aligned. Mark the top square once diagonally from corner to corner. Sew ¼" from both sides of the marked line. Cut on the marked line. Fold open and press the seam allowances toward the lighter fabric to make 144 large triangle squares for the Pinwheel blocks.

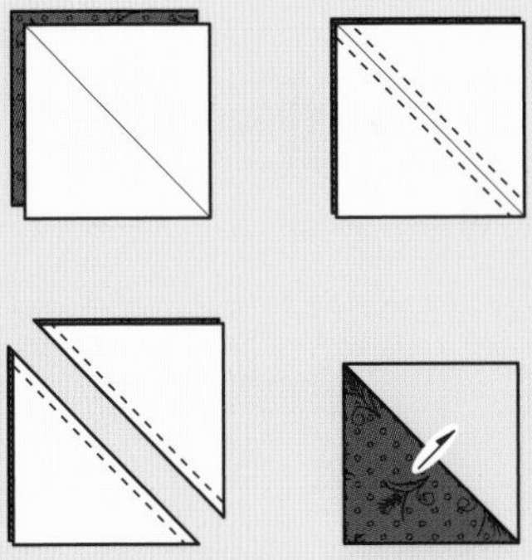

Make 144.

2. Repeat step 1 using the tan print 2⅞" squares and the red print 2⅞" squares to make 76 small triangle squares for the pieced inner border.

Completing the Quilt

Follow the instructions for assembling "Scotch Granny Throw," beginning with "Making the Pinwheel Blocks" on page 93. Use the large triangle squares to make the blocks and the small triangle squares to make the pieced inner border.

PLAN B

From *Save the Scraps* by Gayle Bong. Quilt made by Gayle Bong.

Finished Quilt Size: 54½" x 54½"
Finished Block Size: 9" x 9"

To make this quilt, Gayle used scraps in a rainbow of colors, but this design would be just as effective if it were made in a limited color palette. Folded corners and strip piecing with staggered strip sets make this quilt fast and fun to make, and the end result is truly eye-catching.

Materials

Yardage is based on 42"-wide fabric.

- 2 yards *total* of assorted medium and dark scraps for stars and backgrounds
- 1⅝ yards of dark blue for border and binding
- 1⅜ yards *total* of assorted light scraps for backgrounds (the equivalent of 12 strips, each 3½" x 31")
- ¾ yard *total* of assorted light scraps for stars (the equivalent of 13 strips, each 3½" x 14")
- 3½ yards of fabric for backing
- 60" x 60" piece of batting

Cutting

All measurements include ¼" seam allowances. Instructions are for cutting strips across the fabric width. If you prefer, however, the light pieces don't have to be cut from strips. If you have an assortment of odd-sized scraps, just cut a set of matching light pieces for each block. (For the Light-Star block, cut one 3½" square and four 2⅜" squares. Cut the 2⅜" squares once diagonally to yield 8 half-square triangles. For the Dark-Star block, cut four 3½" squares, four 2" x 3½" rectangles, and four 2" squares.)

From the light scraps for stars, cut:

- 13 strips, 3½" x at least 14"; crosscut *each* strip into:
  - 1 square, 3½" x 3½" (13 squares total)
  - 4 squares, 2⅜" x 2⅜"; cut once diagonally to yield 8 half-square triangles (104 half-square triangles total)

From the medium and dark scraps, cut:

- 36 strips, 2" x 20"
- 52 squares, 2⅜" x 2⅜"; cut once diagonally to yield 104 half-square triangles
- 196 squares, 2" x 2"

From the light scraps for backgrounds, cut:

- 12 strips, 3½" x at least 31"; crosscut *each* strip into:
  - 4 squares, 3½" x 3½" (48 total)
  - 4 rectangles, 2" x 3½" (48 total)
  - 4 squares, 2" x 2" (48 total)

From the dark blue fabric, cut:

- 6 strips, 5" x 42"
- 7 strips, 2¼" x 42"

Making the Light-Star Blocks

Keep each set of matching light fabric pieces together.

1. Join a light triangle and a dark triangle to make a triangle square. Repeat to make a total of 104 squares.

Make 104.

2. Keep each set of eight triangle squares with matching light fabrics together. Sew a pair of triangle squares together as shown. Press the seam allowance open. Repeat to make a total of 52 pairs, keeping the four triangle pairs with matching light fabrics together.

Make 52.

3. Sew medium or dark 2" squares to both ends of two triangle pairs with matching light fabrics from step 2. Sew the remaining two matching triangle pairs to opposite sides of a matching 3½" light square. Sew the rows together as shown to make the light stars. Repeat to make a total of 13 stars.

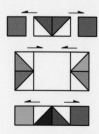

Make 13.

4. Sew the long edges of the 2" x 20" medium and dark strips together into 18 pairs. Press the seams to either side. Sew three pairs of strips together, staggering the ends about 10" as shown. Press the seams to either side. Repeat to

make a total of six staggered sets. Cut the strip sets into 2"-wide segments. You'll need 50 two-square segments and 52 four-square segments. Set aside 24 two-square segments for the centers of the dark stars.

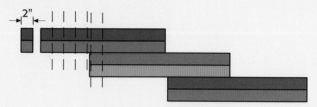

Make 6 sets of 6 strips each.

Cut 50.

Cut 52.

5. Sew two of the four-square segments to opposite sides of a star from step 3. Press the seams away from the star. Repeat to make a total of 13.

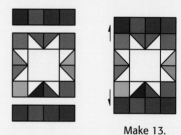

Make 13.

6. Sew a two-square segment to one end of each of the remaining four-square segments. Before pressing, sew the resulting units to the remaining two sides of a star. (If you wait to press, then the seams can be flipped to butt the seams with the center unit seams.) Make a total of 13 Light-Star blocks.

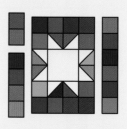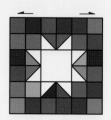

Light-Star block.
Make 13.

Making the Dark-Star Blocks

Keep each set of matching light fabric pieces together.

1. Sew together the two-square segments you set aside in step 4 of "Making the Light-Star Blocks" to make 12 four-patch units.

Make 12.

2. Sew a 2" medium or dark square to a 2" light square; then add a matching 2" x 3½" light rectangle. Repeat to make a total of 48 units.

Make 48.

3. Draw a diagonal line on the wrong side of 96 of the 2" medium or dark squares. Position one of these 2" squares on one corner of a 3½" light square, right sides together. Sew along the diagonal line, trim to ¼" seam allowance, and press the triangle toward the corner. Repeat with another 2" square on the adjacent corner to make the dark-star points. Repeat to make a total of 48 star-point units.

Make 48.

4. Sew a unit from step 2 to each side of a star-point unit from step 3, positioning the units exactly as shown, to make rows 1 and 3 of each block. Sew a star-point unit to each side of a four-patch unit from step 1, positioning the units as shown, to make row 2. All the light fabrics should match. Sew the rows together. Repeat to make a total of 12 Dark-Star blocks.

Row 1
Row 2
Row 3

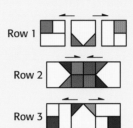 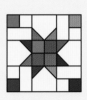

Dark-Star block.
Make 12.

Assembling the Quilt Top

1. Arrange the blocks, alternating Light-Star blocks and Dark-Star blocks as shown in the assembly diagram. Play with the position of the blocks until you are happy with the color arrangement. Sew the blocks into rows, pressing the seams in adjacent rows in opposite directions. Sew the rows together.

2. Referring to "Borders with Mitered Corners" on page 118, sew the 5"-wide dark blue outer-border to the quilt top.

Finishing the Quilt

Refer to "Preparing to Quilt" on page 119, "Quilting Techniques" on page 120, and "Finishing Techniques" on page 121 for more detailed instructions, if needed.

1. Piece the quilt backing so that it is 4" to 6" longer and wider than the quilt top. Mark the quilt top if necessary. Layer the quilt top with batting and backing, and baste the layers together.

2. Hand or machine quilt as desired.

3. Trim the batting and backing even with the edges of the quilt top. Add a hanging sleeve if desired. Using the 2¼"-wide dark blue strips, prepare the binding and sew it to the quilt. Make a label and attach it to your quilt.

LEMOYNE STAR STRING QUILT

From *Everyday Folk Art* by Polly Minick and Laurie Simpson. Quilt made by Laurie Simpson.

Finished Quilt Size: 67½" x 87½"
Finished Block Size: 18" x 18"

This quilt will help put a dent in your stash. Don't be surprised if
it uses up all of your white and beige scraps—and then some!
A timeless pattern and lots of scraps make a "can't-miss" combo.

Materials

Yardage is based on 42"-wide fabric.

- 8 yards *total* of assorted white and beige fabrics
  for blocks and border
- 12 fat quarters of assorted indigo prints for block
  backgrounds
- 2½ yards of indigo fabric for borders and binding
- 5½ yards of backing fabric
- 72" x 92" piece of batting
- Papers for foundation piecing (100-sheet package)

Cutting

All measurements include ¼" seam allowances. Instructions are for cutting strips across the fabric width unless otherwise specified.

From the white and beige fabrics, cut:
- Strips in assorted widths of 1" to 4" and
  lengths of 3" to 5½"
- 2"-wide strips for border, in 3" to 5½" lengths

From *each* of the indigo fat quarters, cut:
- 4 squares, 5¾" x 5¾" (12 matching sets of
  4 each)
- 1 square, 8¾" x 8¾"; cut squares twice diagonally to yield 48 quarter-square triangles

From the indigo fabric, cut on the *lengthwise* grain:
- 2 strips, 3½" x 72½"
- 2 strips, 4½" x 60½"
- 2 strips, 2½" x 83½"
- 2 strips, 2½" x 67½"
- 4 strips, 2¼" x 84"
- Approximately 20 assorted 2" x 2" squares or
  1½" x 2" pieces for border

Making the LeMoyne Star Blocks

Refer to "Foundation Piecing" on page 111 for more detailed information.

1. Photocopy the star-point foundation pattern
   from page 106 onto the sheets of foundation
   paper, and make a total of 96 copies. (You will
   make 12 blocks and each block uses eight star
   points.) Make sure the reproductions are dark
   enough so that the diamond outlines show
   through to the wrong side of the paper. You can
   trace this outline with a pencil onto the other
   side if this is helpful. The tracing doesn't have to
   be perfect—you just want to know roughly
   where the diamond shape is.

2. On the sewing machine, foundation piece the white and beige assorted-width strips to the wrong side of the paper. (The original diamond shape you made on the copy machine is now on the underneath side of the paper.) Begin by laying the first strip of fabric right side up (wrong side against the paper); then lay the next strip on top of the first strip, right sides together and with one long edge aligned with a long edge of the first strip. Stitch approximately ¼" from the raw edges of the strips.

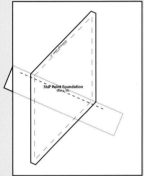
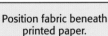
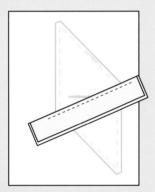

Position fabric beneath printed paper.   Stitch from this side.

3. Flip the top strip open so that both strips are right side up. Press. Continue adding strips of random widths, aligning the edge of each new strip with the last strip added, until the entire diamond shape is covered. Press after the addition of each strip. Make a total of 96 foundation-pieced diamonds.

4. Turn each stitched diamond so that the fabric side is down on your cutting mat. Use a ruler and rotary cutter to trim away the excess paper, making sure to leave a ¼" seam allowance.

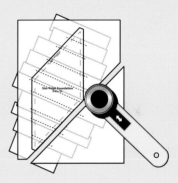

5. If you plan to piece the diamonds together by hand, gently tear the paper off the back of each diamond, taking care not to distort the shape. The paper will tear more easily if you crease it first along the seam line. If you plan to assemble the blocks by machine, you can leave the paper patterns on the diamonds for now and remove them after all the block pieces have been stitched together.

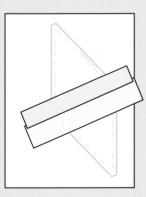
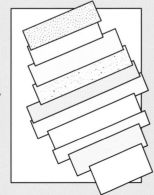

6. Either by hand or by machine, piece together the LeMoyne Star block. First sew the diamonds together in pairs, ending the seam ¼" from the outer end of the diamonds. Sew the pairs together to make half stars, and then sew the halves together, again leaving the last ¼" of each seam open.

7. Select four matching indigo squares and triangles. Sew the corner squares and side triangles in place, leaving the seam allowances free in the corners where the squares and triangles adjoin with two diamonds. Sew from the starting point to the raw edge on each seam.

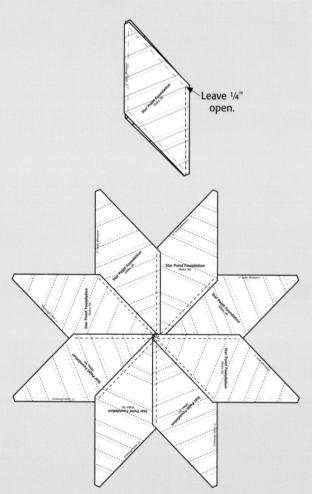

Leave ¼" open.

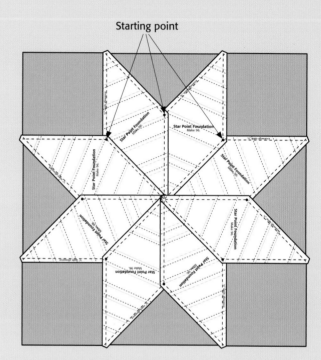

Starting point

8. Repeat steps 6 and 7 to make a total of 12 LeMoyne Star blocks.

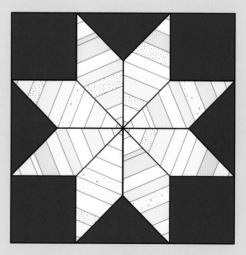

LeMoyne Star block.
Make 12.

Assembling the Quilt-Top Center

Arrange the blocks in four rows of three blocks each. When you are pleased with the arrangement, sew the blocks together into rows, and then sew the rows together. Press.

Adding the Borders

1. Referring to "Borders with Butted Corners" on page 117, attach the 3½" x 72½" indigo strips to the sides of the quilt top and the 4½" x 60½" indigo strips to the top and bottom of the quilt top. Press the seam allowances toward the indigo border

2. To make the middle border, sew the 2"-wide strips of white or beige and the assorted indigo scraps together in a random manner. Make four border strips. Make two strips at least 85" long and two at least 62" long.

3. Attach the two longest middle-border strips to the sides of the quilt top. Trim the strips even with the finished edges of the top. Press the seam allowances toward the indigo border. Attach the other two strips to the top and bottom of the quilt top, and trim and press in the same manner.

4. Attach the 2½"-wide indigo outer border to the quilt top as in step 1.

Finishing the Quilt

Refer to "Preparing to Quilt" on page 119, "Quilting Techniques" on page 120, and "Finishing Techniques" on page 121 for more detailed instructions, if needed.

1. Piece the quilt backing so that it is 4" to 6" longer and wider than the quilt top. Mark the quilt top if necessary. Layer the quilt top with batting and backing, and baste the layers together.

2. Hand or machine quilt as desired.

3. Trim the batting and backing even with the edges of the quilt top. Add a hanging sleeve if desired. Using the 2¼"-wide indigo strips, prepare the binding and sew it to the quilt. Make a label and attach it to your quilt.

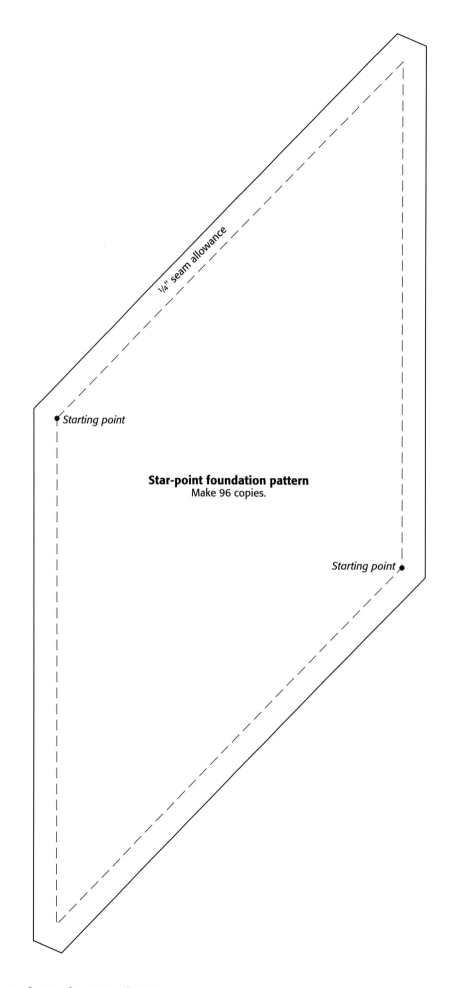

¼" seam allowance

● Starting point

Star-point foundation pattern
Make 96 copies.

Starting point ●

QUILTMAKING BASICS

Whether you're new to quiltmaking or you're simply ready to learn a new technique, you'll find this quiltmaking-basics section filled with helpful information that can make putting your quilt together a pleasurable experience.

Fabrics

Select 100%-cotton fabrics. They hold their shape well and are easy to handle. Cotton blends can be more difficult to stitch and press. Sometimes, however, a cotton blend is worth a little extra effort if it is the perfect fabric for your quilt.

Yardage requirements are provided for all the projects in this book and are based on 42"-wide fabrics that provide at least 40" of usable fabric after prewashing. Some quilts call for an assortment of scraps or can easily be adapted for a scrappy look. If you have a collection of scraps, feel free to use them and purchase only those fabrics you need to complete the quilt you are making.

Supplies

Sewing machine: To machine piece, you'll need a sewing machine that has a good straight stitch. You'll also need a walking foot or darning foot if you will be doing any machine quilting.

Rotary-cutting tools: You will need a rotary cutter, cutting mat, and acrylic ruler. Rotary-cutting rulers are available in a variety of sizes; some of the most frequently used sizes include 6" x 6", 6" x 24", and 12" x 12" or 15" x 15".

Thread: Use a good-quality, all-purpose cotton or cotton-covered polyester thread.

Needles: For machine piecing, a size 10/70 or 12/80 works well for most cottons. For machine quilting and paper piecing, a larger needle, such as a 14/90, works best. For hand appliqué, choose a needle that will glide easily through the edges of the appliqué pieces. Size 10 (fine) to size 12 (very fine) needles work well. For hand quilting, use Betweens, which are short, very sharp needles made specifically for this purpose.

Pins: Long, fine silk pins slip easily through fabric, making them perfect for patchwork. Small sequin pins work well for appliqué, although their shanks are thicker than silk pins.

Scissors: Use your best scissors for cutting fabric only. Use craft scissors to cut paper, fusible web, and template plastic. Sharp embroidery scissors or thread snips are handy for clipping threads.

Template plastic: Use clear or frosted plastic to make durable, accurate templates.

Seam ripper: Use this tool to remove stitches from incorrectly sewn seams.

Marking tools: A variety of tools are available to mark fabric when tracing around templates or marking quilting designs. Use a sharp No. 2 pencil or a fine-lead mechanical pencil on lighter-colored fabrics, and use a silver or chalk pencil on darker fabrics. Chalk pencils or chalk-wheel markers make clear marks on fabric and are easier to remove than grease-based colored pencils. Be sure to test your marking tool to make sure you can remove the marks easily.

Rotary Cutting

Instructions for quick and easy rotary cutting are provided wherever possible. All measurements include standard ¼"-wide seam allowances. If you are unfamiliar with rotary cutting, read the brief introduction below.

1. Fold the fabric and match selvages, aligning the crosswise and lengthwise grains as much as possible. Place the folded edge closest to you on the cutting mat. Align a square ruler along the folded edge of the fabric. Place a long, straight ruler to the left of the square ruler, just covering the uneven raw edges of the left side of the fabric.

    Remove the square ruler and cut along the right edge of the long ruler, rolling the rotary cutter away from you. Discard this strip. (Reverse this procedure if you are left-handed.)

    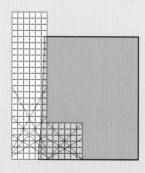

    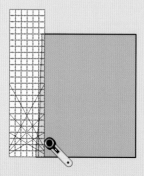

2. To cut strips, align the newly cut edge of the fabric with the ruler markings at the required width. For example, to cut a 3"-wide strip, place the 3" ruler mark on the edge of the fabric.

    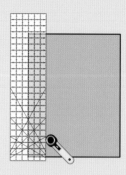

3. To cut squares, cut strips in the required widths. Trim the selvage ends of the strips. Align the left edge of the strips with the correct ruler markings. The sides of the square should have the same measurement as the width of the strips. Cut the strips into squares. Continue cutting squares until you have the number needed.

    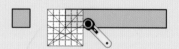

4. To make a half-square triangle, begin by cutting a square ⅞" larger than the desired finished size of the short side of the triangle. Then cut the square once diagonally, from corner to corner. Each square yields two half-square triangles. The short sides of each triangle are on the straight grain of the fabric.

    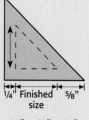

    ¼" Finished 5/8"
    size

    ¼" + 5/8" = 7/8"

5. To make a quarter-square triangle, begin by cutting a square 1¼" larger than the desired finished size of the long edge of the triangle. Then cut the square twice diagonally, from corner to corner. Each square yields four quarter-square triangles. The long side of each triangle is on the straight grain of the fabric.

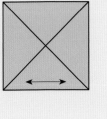

⁵⁄₈" Finished ⁵⁄₈"
size

⁵⁄₈" + ⁵⁄₈" = 1¼"

Machine Piecing

Most blocks in this book are designed for easy rotary cutting and quick piecing. Some blocks, however, require the use of templates for particular shapes, such as "Triangle Swirls" on page 20. Templates for machine piecing include the required ¼"-wide seam allowances. Cut out the templates on the outside lines so that they include the seam allowances. Be sure to mark the pattern name and grain-line arrow on each template.

The most important thing to remember about machine piecing is that you need to maintain a consistent ¼"-wide seam allowance. Otherwise, the quilt blocks won't be the desired finished size. If that happens, the size of everything else in the quilt is affected, including alternate blocks, sashings, and borders. Measurements for all components of each quilt are based on blocks that finish accurately to the desired size plus ¼" on each edge for seam allowances.

Take the time to establish an exact ¼"-wide seam guide on your machine. Some machines have a special presser foot that measures exactly ¼" from the center needle position to the edge of the foot.

This feature allows you to use the edge of the presser foot to guide the fabric for a perfect ¼"-wide seam allowance.

If your machine doesn't have such a foot, create a seam guide by placing the edge of a piece of tape, moleskin, or a magnetic seam guide ¼" away from the needle.

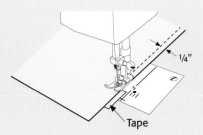

¼"

Tape

Chain Piecing

Chain piecing is an efficient system that saves time and thread. It's especially useful when you're making many identical units.

1. Sew the first pair of pieces from cut edge to cut edge, using 12 to 15 stitches per inch. At the end of the seam, stop sewing but don't cut the thread.

2. Feed the next pair of pieces under the presser foot, as close as possible to the first. Continue feeding pieces through the machine without cutting the threads in between the pairs.

3. When all the pieces are sewn, remove the chain from the machine and clip the threads between the pairs of sewn pieces.

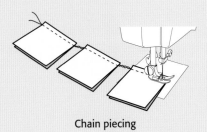

Chain piecing

Triangle Squares

A triangle square is made up of two half-square triangles sewn together. Here is a method of making triangle squares that is fast and accurate.

1. Cut the squares the size specified in the cutting list.

2. Draw a diagonal line from corner to corner on the wrong side of the lighter fabric. Layer two same-sized squares right sides together with the marked square on top and raw edges aligned. Sew ¼" on each side of the drawn diagonal line.

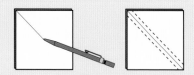

3. Cut on the drawn line. Press the seams toward the darker fabric unless instructed otherwise, and trim the dog-ears. Each pair of squares will yield two triangle squares.

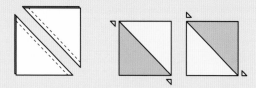

4. If your triangle squares need to be trimmed, use a square ruler to trim them to the correct unfinished size. Place the diagonal line of the ruler on the seam of the triangle square and trim two sides as shown. Rotate the block and trim the other two sides.

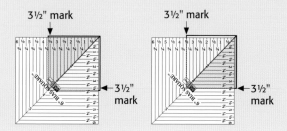

Quarter-Square-Triangle Units

These pieced squares are made up of four quarter-square triangles sewn together. Here are two methods of making these pieced squares that are quick and accurate.

Quick Sew and Cut Method

1. Draw intersecting diagonal lines from corner to corner on the wrong side of the lighter fabric as shown. Layer two same-sized squares right sides together with the marked square on top and raw edges aligned.

2. Stitch ¼" from the drawn lines as shown, making sure to stop stitching where the lines intersect. Also, as you rotate the squares to stitch each subsequent seam, make sure that you're always stitching on the same side of the marked line (either always on the right or always on the left) as shown.

3. Cut along the drawn lines and press the resulting triangles open. At this point you can sew these two units together to make a quarter-square-triangle unit, or you can make many from different fabrics and mix them up.

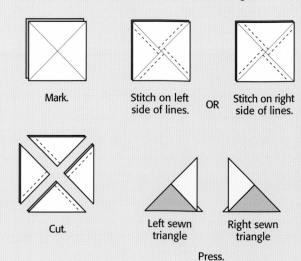

Two Triangle Squares Method

1. Cut two squares that are 1½" larger than the desired finished square. For example, to make a 3" finished quarter-square-triangle unit, start with 4½" squares.

2. Referring to "Triangle Squares" on page 110, draw a diagonal line on the wrong side of one square, usually the lighter one, and place the squares right sides together. Stitch ¼" from the line on each side. Cut on the drawn line and press the seam allowances toward the darker fabric. You will have two triangle squares. Don't trim your squares to size yet.

3. On the wrong side of one of the triangle squares, draw a diagonal line from corner to corner as shown.

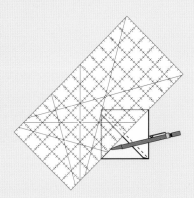

4. Place the triangle squares right sides together. Make sure contrasting fabrics are facing each other and that the marked square is on top. Butt the diagonal seams against each other and pin to secure. Stitch ¼" from both sides of the marked diagonal line; then cut on the drawn line. Press the seams toward one side. You will have two quarter-square-triangle units.

5. Now you are ready to trim your units. For example, if you would like a 3" finished unit (3½" unfinished), place the diagonal line of the square ruler on one of the seam lines. Move the ruler along the seam line until the 3½" mark on both sides of the ruler lines up where the two fabrics intersect. Trim along both edges of the ruler. Rotate your unit and trim the other two sides so that your unfinished piece is 3½". This may take a little more effort, but your quarter-square-triangle units will be perfectly sized.

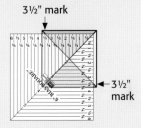

Trim first two sides.

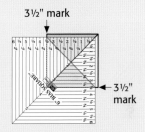

Trim remaining two sides.

NOTE: *If you are very accurate with your stitching and wish to avoid trimming, cut the squares 1¼" larger than the desired finished size of the quarter-square-triangle unit, rather than 1½" larger.*

Foundation Piecing

1. Begin by making copies of the pattern. You can do this either by hand or on a copy machine. Make one copy and compare it to the original for accuracy. If your copy machine produces an accurate reproduction, make as many photocopies as the pattern calls for. Only make copies from the original, because the pattern may become distorted if you make copies of a copy.

Use a rotary cutter and ruler to trim the excess paper around the pattern. If you are tracing the copies by hand, transfer all interior lines and numbers on the pattern to your copy.

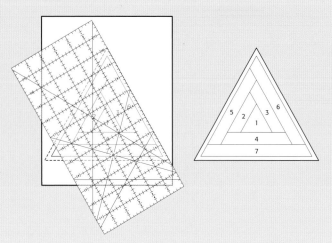

2. Following the project instructions, cut the fabric pieces for each block. The measurements listed for the individual pieces are slightly larger than needed. (It's better to have too much fabric to cut away than not enough to cover the area.)

3. Shorten the stitch length on your sewing machine. A short stitch will make it easier to remove the papers after the blocks are sewn.

4. Many foundation-piecing patterns will have numbered segments or areas. If they do, you will add the pieces in numerical order. Hold the pattern with the printed or numbered side facing you. Place the wrong side of the fabric for piece 1 on the unprinted side of the pattern, centering the fabric over area 1. You can hold the paper up to a light to help position the fabric properly. Make sure the fabric piece not only covers the entire area 1 but also extends at least ¼" beyond the area 1 lines. Place the fabric for piece 2 right sides together with piece 1 so that there is approximately a ¼" seam allowance extending into area 2. If you flip the pattern over, the right side of piece 1 and the wrong side of piece 2 will be facing up. You can pin the pieces to the paper, but if you do, be

certain that you place the pin so that it does not extend into the seam line.

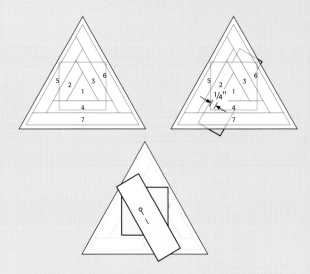

5. Place the pattern with the printed side facing up on your sewing machine. The fabric will be beneath the paper. Start sewing a couple of stitches before the seam line, and then sew directly along the seam line between areas 1 and 2. You will stitch through the paper and fabric layers. Stop stitching a couple of stitches beyond the line. There is no need to backstitch.

6. With the fabric facing you, fold the paper back and out of the way. Trim the seam to approximately ¼" and press. Sometimes the ink on photocopied paper will transfer onto your ironing board, so use a pressing cloth when ironing.

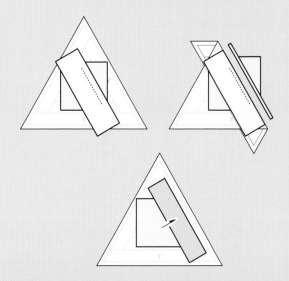

7. Repeating the procedure used in steps 4–6, continue sewing pieces to the block in numerical order until all areas of the pattern are complete. On the outermost pieces, begin and end the seam ¼" beyond the ends of the pattern lines.

8. Trim each block to the edge of the paper (¼" from the outside stitching lines on the pattern).

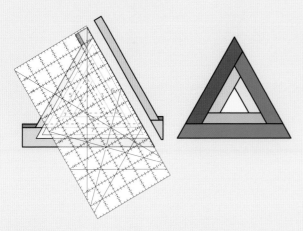

9. Tear the paper off your blocks before piecing them together unless instructed to do otherwise.

Easing

If two pieces being sewn together are slightly different in size (less than ⅛"), pin the places where the two pieces should match, and in between if necessary, to distribute the excess fabric evenly. Sew the seam with the larger piece on the bottom. The feed dogs will ease the two pieces together.

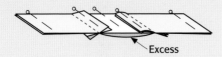

Excess

Pressing

The traditional rule in quiltmaking is to press seams to one side, toward the darker color wherever possible. First press the seams flat from the wrong side of the fabric; then press the seams in the desired direction from the right side. Press carefully to avoid distorting the shapes.

When joining two seamed units, plan ahead and press the seam allowances in opposite directions, as shown. This reduces bulk and makes it easier to match the seams. The seam allowances will butt against each other where two seams meet, making it easier to sew units with perfectly matched seam intersections.

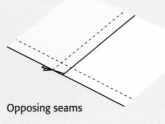

Opposing seams

Appliqué Basics

General instructions are provided here for needle-turn, freezer-paper, and fusible appliqué. Even when a specific method of appliqué is mentioned in a project, you are always free to substitute your favorite method. Just be sure to adapt the pattern pieces and project instructions as necessary.

Making Templates

To begin, you will need to make templates of the appliqué patterns. Templates made from clear plastic are durable and since you can see through the plastic, it is easy to trace the templates accurately from the book page.

Place template plastic over each pattern piece and trace with a fine-line permanent marker. Don't add seam allowances. Cut out the templates on the drawn lines. You need only one template for each different motif or shape. Write the pattern name and grain-line arrow (if applicable) on the template.

Appliquéing by Hand

In traditional hand appliqué, the seam allowances are turned under before the appliqué is stitched to the background fabric. Two traditional methods for turning under the edges are needle-turn appliqué and freezer-paper appliqué. You can use either method to turn under the raw edges, and then use the traditional appliqué stitch to attach the shapes to your background fabric.

Needle-Turn Appliqué

1. Using a plastic template, trace the design onto the right side of the appliqué fabric. Use a No. 2 pencil to mark light fabrics and a white pencil to mark dark fabrics.

2. Cut out the fabric piece, adding a scant ¼"-wide seam allowance all around the marked shape.

3. Position the appliqué piece on the background fabric. Pin or baste in place. If the pieces are numbered, start with piece 1 and add the remaining pieces in numerical order.

4. Starting on a straight edge, use the tip of the needle to gently turn under the seam allowance, about ½" at a time. Hold the turned seam allowance firmly between the thumb and first finger of one hand as you stitch the appliqué to the background fabric with your other hand. Use a longer needle—a Sharp or milliner's needle—to help you control the seam allowance and turn it under neatly. Use the traditional appliqué stitch to sew your appliqué pieces to the background. See "Traditional Appliqué Stitch" on page 115.

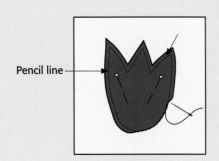

Pencil line

Freezer-Paper Appliqué

Freezer paper, which is coated on one side, is often used to help make perfectly shaped appliqués.

1. Trace around the plastic template on the paper side (not the shiny side) of the freezer paper with a sharp pencil, or place the freezer paper, shiny side down, on top of the pattern and trace.

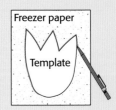

Freezer paper

Template

2. Cut out the traced design on the pencil line. Don't add seam allowances.

3. With the shiny side of the paper against the wrong side of your appliqué fabric, iron the freezer-paper cutout in place with a hot, dry iron.

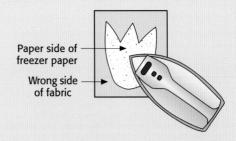

Paper side of freezer paper

Wrong side of fabric

4. Cut out the fabric shape, adding ¼" seam allowances all around the outside edge of the freezer paper.

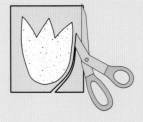

5. Turn and baste the seam allowance over the freezer-paper edges by hand, or use a fabric glue stick. Clip inside points and fold outside points.

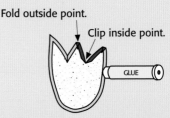

Fold outside point.

Clip inside point.

GLUE

6. Pin or baste the design to the background fabric or block. If the pieces are numbered, start with piece 1 and add the remaining pieces in numerical order. Appliqué the design with the traditional appliqué stitch. See "Traditional Appliqué Stitch" below.

7. Remove any basting stitches. Cut a slit in the background fabric behind the appliqué and remove the freezer paper with tweezers. If you used a glue stick, soak the piece in warm water for a few minutes before removing the freezer paper.

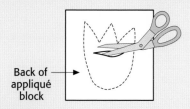

Back of appliqué block

Traditional Appliqué Stitch

The traditional appliqué stitch or blindstitch is appropriate for sewing all appliqué shapes, including sharp points and curves.

1. Thread the needle with a single strand of thread that is approximately 18" long in a color that closely matches the color of your appliqué. Knot the thread tail.

2. Hide the knot by slipping the needle into the seam allowance from the wrong side of the appliqué piece, bringing it out on the fold line.

3. Work from right to left if you are right-handed, or from left to right if you are left-handed. To make the first stitch, insert the needle into the background right next to where the needle came out of the appliqué fabric. Bring the needle up through the edge of the appliqué, about ⅛" from the first stitch.

4. As you bring the needle up, pierce the basted edge of the appliqué piece, catching only one or two threads.

5. Again, take a stitch into the background fabric right next to where the thread came up through the appliqué. Bring the needle up about ⅛" from the previous stitch, again catching the basted edge of the appliqué.

6. Give the thread a slight tug and continue stitching.

   NOTE: *The stitches in the appliqué illustration are drawn large to indicate placement. The stitches should not show in the completed work.*

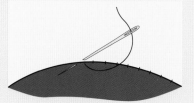

Appliqué stitch

7. To end your stitching, pull the needle through to the wrong side. Behind the appliqué piece, take two small stitches, making knots by taking your needle through the loops.

Fusible Appliqué

Using fusible web is a fast and fun way to appliqué. If the appliqué pattern is directional, you need to make a reverse tracing of the pattern so that the pattern will match the original design when fused in place. Otherwise, your finished project will be the reverse of the project shown in the book. You don't need to make reverse tracings for patterns that are symmetrical or for ones that are already printed in reverse, such as the patterns for "Fresh Flowers" on page 58.

Refer to the manufacturer's directions when applying fusible web to your fabrics; each brand is a little different and pressing it too long may result in fusible web that doesn't stick well.

1. Trace or draw your shape on the paper backing side of the fusible web. Cut out the shape, leaving about a ¼" margin all around the outline.

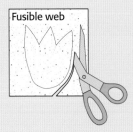

Fusible web

2. Fuse shapes to the wrong side of your fabric.

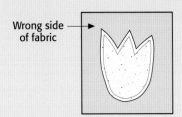

Wrong side of fabric

3. Cut out the shape exactly on the marked line.

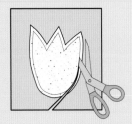

4. Remove the paper backing, position the shape on the background, and press it in place with your iron. If the pieces are numbered, start with piece 1 and add the remaining pieces in numerical order.

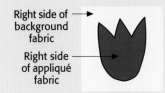

Right side of background fabric

Right side of appliqué fabric

5. If desired, you can add decorative stitches by hand or machine around the edges of the fused appliqués. Commonly used stitches include satin stitch and blanket stitch.

Making Bias Stems

Bias stems are easy to make with the help of metal or nylon bias press bars. These handy notions are available at most quilt shops and come in sets of assorted widths. The projects in this book use ¼" and ½" bias bars. The following steps describe the process of making bias stems.

1. Cut a piece of fabric as instructed in the specific quilt instructions. For a ½" bias stem, you'll need to cut the fabric into 1¼"-wide bias strips with a rotary cutter and clear acrylic ruler.

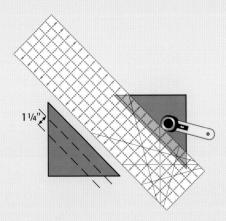

1 ¼"

2. Fold each strip in half lengthwise, wrong sides together. Stitch ½" from the folded edge. This will leave a ⅛" seam allowance.

Fold

½"

⅛" seam allowance

3. Insert a ½" bias bar, roll the seam so it is centered along one flat edge of the bias bar, and press flat. Remove the bias bar. The finished strip will measure ½" wide.

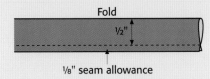

Bias bar

Squaring Up Blocks

When your blocks are complete, take the time to square them up. Use a large square ruler to measure your blocks and make sure they are the desired size plus an exact ¼" seam allowance on each side. For example, if you are making 9" blocks, they should all measure 9½" before you sew them together. Trim the larger blocks to match the size of the smallest one. Be sure to trim all four sides, or your block will be lopsided.

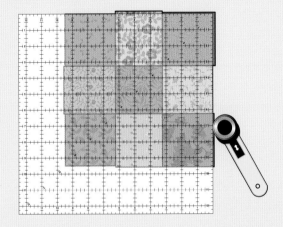

If your blocks aren't the required finished size, adjust all the other components of the quilt, such as sashing and borders, accordingly.

Adding Borders

For best results, don't cut border strips and sew them directly to the quilt without measuring first. The edges of a quilt often measure slightly longer than the distance through the quilt center, due to stretching during construction. Instead, measure the quilt top through the center in both directions to determine how long to cut the border strips. This step ensures that the finished quilt will be as straight and as square as possible, without wavy edges.

Many of the quilts in this book call for plain border strips. These strips generally are cut along the crosswise grain and seamed where extra length is needed. However, some projects call for the borders to be cut on the lengthwise grain so that they don't need to be pieced.

Borders may have butted corners, corner squares, or mitered corners. Check the quilt pattern you are following to see which type of corner treatment you need.

Borders with Butted Corners

1. Measure the length of the quilt top through the center. From the crosswise grain, cut border strips to that measurement, piecing as necessary. Determine the midpoints of the border and quilt top by folding in half and creasing or pinning the centers. Then pin the border strips to opposite sides of the quilt top, matching the center marks and ends and easing as necessary. Sew the border strips in place. Press the seams toward the border strips.

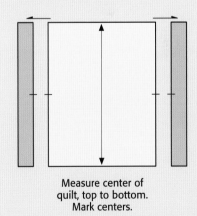

Measure center of
quilt, top to bottom.
Mark centers.

2. Measure the width of the quilt top through the center, including the side border strips just added. From the crosswise grain, cut border strips to that measurement, piecing as necessary. Mark the centers of the quilt edges and the border strips. Pin the border strips to the top and bottom edges of the quilt top, matching the center marks and ends and easing as necessary.

Sew the border strips in place. Press the seams toward the border strips.

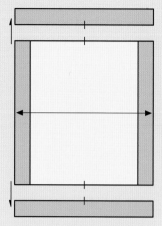

Measure center of quilt, side to side, including border strips. Mark centers.

Borders with Corner Squares

1. Measure the width and length of the quilt top through the center.

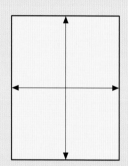

Measure center of quilt top in both directions.

2. From the crosswise grain, cut border strips to those measurements, piecing as necessary. Mark the centers of the quilt edges and the border strips. Pin the side border strips to opposite sides of the quilt top, matching centers and ends and easing as necessary. Sew the side border strips to the quilt top; press the seam allowances toward the border strips.

3. Cut corner squares of the required size, which is the cut width of the border strips. Sew a corner square to each end of the remaining two border strips; press the seam allowances toward the border strips. Pin the border strips to the top and bottom edges of the quilt top. Match the centers, seams between the border strips and corner squares, and ends. Ease as necessary and stitch. Press the seam allowances toward the border strips.

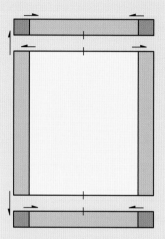

Borders with Mitered Corners

1. Estimate the finished outside dimensions of your quilt, including the border. For example, if your quilt top measures 35½" x 50½" across the center and you want a 5"-wide border, your quilt will measure about 45" x 60" after the border is attached. Add at least ½" to these measurements for seam allowances. To give yourself some leeway, you may want to add an additional 3" to 4" to those measurements. In this example, you would then cut two border strips that measure approximately 48" long and two border strips that measure approximately 63" long.

    NOTE: *If your quilt has more than one border, you can sew all the border strips together for each side first and then sew them all to the quilt top at once. When you are mitering the corners, be sure to match the seam intersections of each different border.*

2. Fold the quilt in half and mark the centers of the quilt edges. Fold each border strip in half and mark the centers with pins.

3. Measure the length and width of the quilt top across the center. Note the measurements.

4. Place a pin at each end of the side border strips to mark the length of the quilt top. Repeat with the top and bottom border strips.

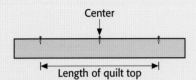

Center

Length of quilt top

5. Pin the border strips to the quilt top, matching the centers. Line up the pins at either end of the border strip with the edges of the quilt. Stitch, beginning and ending ¼" from the raw edges of the quilt top. Repeat with the remaining border strips.

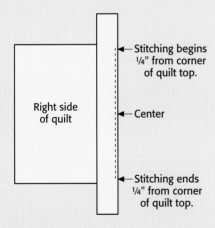

Stitching begins ¼" from corner of quilt top.

Right side of quilt

Center

Stitching ends ¼" from corner of quilt top.

6. Lay the first corner to be mitered on the ironing board. Fold under one border strip at a 45° angle to the other strip. Press and pin.

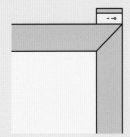

7. Fold the quilt with right sides together, lining up the adjacent edges of the border. If necessary, use a ruler and pencil to draw a line on the crease to make the stitching line more visible. Stitch on the pressed crease, sewing from the previous stitching line to the outside edges.

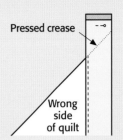

Pressed crease

Wrong side of quilt

8. Press the seam open, check the right side of the quilt to make sure the miters are neat, and then turn the quilt over and trim away the excess border strips, leaving a ¼" seam allowance.

9. Repeat with the remaining corners.

Preparing to Quilt

If you'll be quilting your project by hand or on your home sewing machine, you'll want to follow these directions for marking, layering, basting, and quilting. However, if you plan to have a professional machine quilter quilt your project, check with that person before preparing your finished quilt top in any way. Quilts don't need to be layered and basted for long-arm machine quilting, nor do they usually need to be marked.

Marking the Design

Whether you mark quilting designs on the quilt top or not depends upon the type of quilting you will be doing. Marking is not necessary if you plan to quilt in the ditch (along the seam lines) or outline quilt a uniform distance from seam lines. For more complex quilting designs, however, mark the quilt top before the quilt is layered with batting and backing.

Choose a marking tool that will be visible on your fabric and test it on fabric scraps to be sure the marks can be removed easily. See "Marking tools" on page 107 for options.

Layering and Basting the Quilt

Once you complete the quilt top and mark it for quilting, assemble the quilt "sandwich," which consists of the backing, batting, and the quilt top. The quilt backing and batting should be at least 4" to 6" longer and wider than the quilt top. For large quilts, it is usually necessary to sew two or three lengths of fabric together to make a backing that is large enough. Trim away the selvages before piecing the lengths together. Press the seams open to make quilting easier.

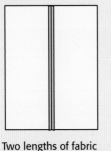 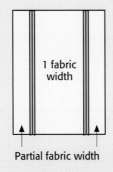

Two lengths of fabric seamed in the center

1 fabric width

Partial fabric width

1. Spread the backing wrong side up on a flat, clean surface. Anchor it with pins or masking tape. Be careful not to stretch the backing out of shape.

2. Spread the batting over the backing, smoothing out any wrinkles.

3. Center the pressed quilt top on top of the batting. Smooth out any wrinkles and make sure the quilt-top edges are parallel to the edges of the backing.

4. Starting in the center, baste with needle and thread and work diagonally to each corner. Then baste a grid of horizontal and vertical lines 6" to 8" apart. Finish by basting around the edges.

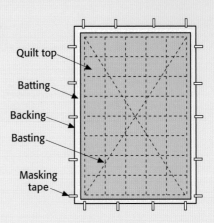

Quilt top

Batting

Backing

Basting

Masking tape

NOTE: *For machine quilting, you can baste the layers with #2 rustproof safety pins. Place pins about 6" to 8" apart, away from the areas you intend to quilt.*

Quilting Techniques

Some of the projects in this book were hand quilted, others were machine quilted, and some were quilted on long-arm quilting machines. The choice is yours!

Hand Quilting

To quilt by hand, you will need short, sturdy needles (called Betweens), quilting thread, and a thimble to fit the middle finger of your sewing hand. Most quilters also use a frame or hoop to support their work. Use the smallest needle you can comfortably handle; the finer the needle, the smaller your stitches will be. The basics of hand quilting are explained below. For more information on hand quilting, refer to *Loving Stitches: A Guide to Fine Hand Quilting* by Jeana Kimball (Martingale & Company, 2003).

1. Thread your needle with a single strand of quilting thread about 18" long. Make a small knot and insert the needle in the top layer about 1" from the place where you want to start stitching. Pull the needle out at the point where quilting will begin and gently pull the thread until the knot pops through the fabric and into the batting.

2. Take small, evenly spaced stitches through all three quilt layers. Rock the needle up and down through all layers, until you have three or four stitches on the needle. Place your other hand underneath the quilt so that you can feel the needle point with the tip of your finger when a stitch is taken.

3. To end a line of quilting, make a small knot close to the last stitch. Then backstitch, running the thread a needle's length through the batting. Gently pull the thread until the knot pops into the batting; clip the thread at the quilt's surface.

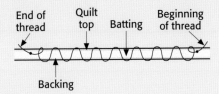

Machine Quilting

Machine quilting is suitable for all types of quilts, from wall hangings to crib quilts to full-size bed quilts. With machine quilting, you can quickly complete quilts that might otherwise languish on the shelves of your sewing room.

Marking the quilting design is necessary only if you need to follow a grid or a complex pattern. It's not necessary if you plan to quilt in the ditch, outline quilt a uniform distance from seam lines, or free-motion quilt in a random pattern.

For straight-line quilting, it is extremely helpful to have a walking foot to help feed the quilt layers through the machine without shifting or puckering. Some machines have a built-in walking foot; others require a separate attachment.

For free-motion quilting, you need a darning foot and the ability to drop or cover the feed dogs on your machine. With free-motion quilting, you guide the fabric in the direction of the design rather than turning the fabric under the needle. Use free-motion quilting to outline quilt a motif or to create stippling or other curved designs.

Professional Quilting

If you prefer to have your quilt quilted by a professional, ask at your local quilt shop for references about someone in your area who does this type of work.

Finishing Techniques

Bind your quilt, add a hanging sleeve if one is needed, label your quilt, and you're finished!

Binding

If your quilt is going to receive moderate to heavy use, add a double-fold binding, which uses two thicknesses of fabric. If your quilt is a wall hanging or will be used very little, a single-fold binding made with one thickness of fabric should be just fine. If you would like your quilt to have a hanging sleeve, see "Adding a Hanging Sleeve" on page 124 before you sew on your binding.

Double-Fold Binding

For a double-fold binding, cut strips 2" to 2½" wide across the width of the fabric. (Some quilters prefer narrow binding, especially if a low-loft batting is used. If you're using a thicker batting, you may want to use 2½"-wide strips.) You will need enough strips to go around the perimeter of the quilt, plus 10" for seams and to turn the corners.

1. Sew the binding strips together to make one long strip. Join strips at right angles, right sides together, and stitch across the corner, as shown. Trim excess fabric and press the seams open to make one long piece of binding.

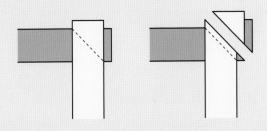

2. Fold the strip in half lengthwise, wrong sides together, and press.

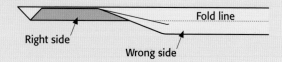

Fold line

Right side

Wrong side

3. Trim the batting and backing even with the quilt top. If you plan to add a hanging sleeve, do so now before attaching the binding (see page 124).

4. Starting on one side of the quilt and using a ¼"-wide seam allowance, stitch the binding to the quilt, keeping the raw edges even with the quilt-top edge, and leaving a 6" tail unstitched where you start. End the stitching ¼" from the corner of the quilt and backstitch. Clip the thread.

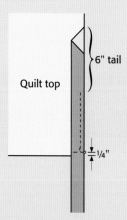

6" tail

Quilt top

¼"

5. Turn the quilt so that you will be stitching down the next side. Fold the binding straight up, away from the quilt, making a 45° angle. Fold the binding back down onto itself, even with the edge of the quilt top. Begin stitching ¼" from the corner, backstitching to secure the stitches. Repeat the process on the remaining edges and corners of the quilt.

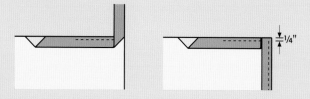

¼"

6. On the last side of the quilt, stop stitching about 7" from where you began. Remove the quilt from the machine. Overlap the ending binding tail with the starting tail. Trim the binding ends with a perpendicular cut so that the overlap is exactly the same distance as the cut width of your binding strips. (If your binding strips are 2½" wide, the overlap should be 2½"; for 2"-wide binding, the overlap should be 2".)

2½" overlap

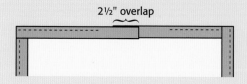

7. Open up the two ends of folded binding. Place the tails right sides together so that they join to form a right angle, as shown. Mark a diagonal stitching line from corner to corner and then pin the binding tails together.

Draw diagonal line.
Pin ends together.

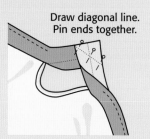

8. Stitch the binding tails together on the marked line. Trim the seam allowance to ¼"; press the seam open to reduce bulk. Refold the binding, align the edges with the raw edges of the quilt top, and finish sewing it in place.

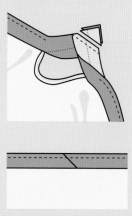

9. Fold the binding over the raw edges to the back of the quilt, with the folded edge covering the row of machine stitching. Hand stitch in place, mitering the corners.

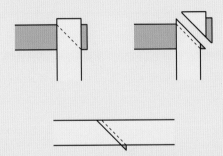

Quilt back

Single-Fold Binding

1. Sew the binding strips together at a 45° angle as shown and press the seams to one side.

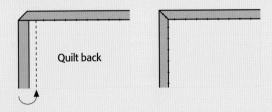

2. Fold over ¼" at one end of the binding strip and press, wrong sides together. Starting with the folded end, position the binding on the quilt, right sides together, and align the raw edges. Stitch the binding to the quilt top, starting at the center of one side and using a ¼" seam. Sew through all three layers. Stop ¼" from the first corner and backstitch.

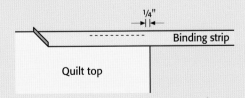

¼"

Binding strip

Quilt top

3. Remove the quilt from the machine. Turn the quilt and fold the binding straight up, making a 45° angle. Fold the binding back down, aligning it with the edge of the next side. Continue sewing the remaining sides in this way. When you come to the place where you started, stitch over the end you folded at the beginning and clip the excess.

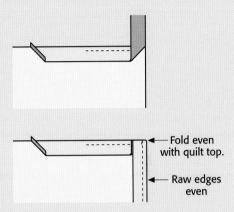

Fold even with quilt top.

Raw edges even

4. Fold the binding over the raw edges to the back of the quilt. Turn the raw edge under ¼" and slip-stitch it to the back of the quilt using matching thread. Miter each of the corners as shown.

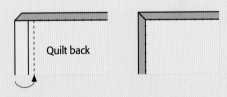

Quilt back

Adding a Hanging Sleeve

If you plan to display your finished quilt on the wall, be sure to add a hanging sleeve to hold the rod.

1. Using leftover fabric from the quilt backing, cut a strip 6" to 8" wide and 1" shorter than the width of your quilt. Fold the ends under ½", and then ½" again to make a hem. Stitch in place.

Fold ends under ½" twice.

2. Fold the fabric strip in half lengthwise, wrong sides together, and baste the raw edges to the top of the quilt back. The top edge of the sleeve will be secured when the binding is sewn on the quilt.

Baste sleeve to top edge of quilt.

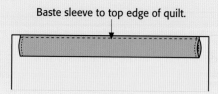

3. Finish the sleeve after the binding has been attached by blindstitching the bottom of the sleeve in place. Push the bottom edge of the sleeve up just a bit to provide a little give; this will keep the hanging rod from putting strain on the quilt.

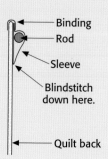

Binding
Rod
Sleeve
Blindstitch down here.
Quilt back

Signing Your Quilt

Be sure to sign and date your quilt. Future generations will be interested to know more than just who made it and when. Labels can be as elaborate or as simple as you desire. The information can be handwritten, typed, or embroidered. Be sure to include the name of the quilt, your name, your city and state, the date, the name of the recipient (if the quilt is a gift), and any other interesting or important information about the quilt.

ABOUT THE CONTRIBUTORS

Laurie Bevan

"Bright Bouquets," page 66

Laurie has been quilting for more than 12 years, and her favorite quilts are traditional pieced ones. She recently wrote her first book, *Lickety-Split Quilts.* Laurie currently works as a freelance technical editor for Martingale & Company, having fun working on other authors' books as well as her own. Laurie's newest venture is a quilter's retreat house that she opened in Poulsbo, Washington, near her home on the beautiful Hood Canal shoreline.

Gayle Bong

"Plan B," page 96

Gayle started quilting in 1981. Designing quilts and writing patterns comes naturally to her; she's always been attracted to geometric patterns, fabric, math, puzzles, and writing. She developed unique concepts for designing and cutting quilts, and authored books on these concepts. She especially loves sharing the excitement of quilting with her students and at guild programs. In her spare time she enjoys gardening, and hiking in the fields and wooded hills around her rural home in Wisconsin. This quilt is from her book *Save the Scraps.*

Jayme Crow and Joan Segna

"Log Cabin Polka," page 71

This quilt is from Jayme and Joan's second book, *Follow the Dots . . . to Dazzling Quilts.* Their first book was *Stitch and Split Appliqué.*

Jayme's passion for quilting has grown out of a love for combining color, design, and fabrics. She enjoys teaching and learning from others to expand her knowledge of textile and design. While indulging in her delight for gardening, she often dreams up new ideas to try in the design studio.

Joan has studied all aspects of fiber, including weaving, tailoring, and fiber art. She studied art and design in college and studied oil painting for six years. Quilting is the perfect blend of her love of art, design, color, and fabric.

In the fall of 1999, Jayme and Joan launched their business, Bella Nonna Design Studio, and in 2001, they displayed their first line of quilt patterns at International Quilt Market. Since then, they have enjoyed expanding their niche in the quilting world.

Nancy Mahoney

"Nantucket Baskets," page 14

This quilt is from Nancy's most recent book, *Basket Bonanza.* Her previous books include *Pairing Up* and *Patchwork Showcase.*

Nancy has been actively quilting since 1987, and since then her quilts have been featured in many quilt books and national quilt magazines. She enjoys the art of quiltmaking and believes that each quilt is a fun and exciting learning experience. Nancy likes to use traditional blocks to create quilts that look complex but are easy to make using updated techniques. When she's not quilting, she enjoys gardening, walking on the beach, and shopping for antiques.

Rosemary Makhan

"Road to Paradise," page 43

A traditional quiltmaker, Rosemary loves appliqué and makes many pieced quilts as well. She especially loves sampler quilts that are based on a theme, such as her quilts in *Biblical Blocks* and *More Biblical Quilt Blocks*. Often the quilts Rosemary makes are her own design. If they are not, she changes or adds something to make them distinctive. She has created many patterns printed under her own pattern label, Quilts by Rose-mary. Each fall, Rosemary helps conduct a Quilting in the Country retreat for quilters in the picturesque Ontario countryside. This quilt is from *More Biblical Quilt Blocks*.

Polly Minick and Laurie Simpson

"LeMoyne Star String Quilt," page 101

Polly and Laurie are sisters who have authored two books together. Their first book was *Folk Art Friends*. This quilt is from their second book, *Everyday Folk Art*.

Polly began hooking rugs in the late 1970s. Like early-American rug hookers, she draws inspiration from her love of home, family, nature, and country. This shows in her imagery, which includes houses, horses, hearts, flags, stars, and birds. Her style is commonly described as "primitive, almost childlike," which places strong emphasis on her respect and solemn appreciation for early-American creations.

For more than 30 years, Laurie has delighted others with her quilts. Drawn to traditional themes and techniques, she pieces, appliqués, and quilts exclusively by hand. "I quilt in the car and at hockey games. Handwork is calming and meditative. It's the way I was meant to work," says Laurie.

These sisters agree that one of the benefits of authoring books is the enjoyment of getting to work together. In addition, they are excited about promoting fiber art as a true art form and encouraging others to follow their lead.

Anne Moscicki and Linda Wyckoff-Hickey

"Scotch Granny Quilt," page 88, and "Scotch Granny Throw," page 92

Anne's childhood interests in arts and crafts led her to combine a love of quilting with her award-winning career as an art director for print media.

Linda picked up a needle and thread at age six and never put them down as she began to design and sell unique clothing and custom-made quilts.

Together they began Touchwood Quilt Design to create designs for quilters like themselves: busy women who place high value on their families and time, and enjoy creating projects that reflect personal style. These quilts are from their first book together, *Joined at the Heart*.

Karen Murphy

"Triangle Swirls," page 20

This quilt is from Karen's first book, *Log Cabin Quilts*.

Karen has been sewing since she was nine years old, making her own clothes and then the clothes for her children. When they were old enough to want clothes from the mall, Karen's textile interest changed to quilting. She taught herself to quilt, at first using garment-construction "rules" until she quickly found out that quilting has different rules. That first project took Karen more than a year to complete, but every year she improved her technique and speed. She has sold many quilts at craft shows and fairs, and after a few years wanted more control over the design of her quilts and began her own pattern company, Idaho Quilt Company.

Claudia Olson

"Interlocked Mosaic Stars," page 26

This quilt is from Claudia's book *Two-Block Appliqué Quilts.*

Claudia began quilting more than 18 years ago under the instruction of Marsha McCloskey, who inspired her to make two-block quilts. She soon began teaching quilting classes and found that she enjoyed the role of encouraging new quilters. Claudia began designing quilts and creating patterns in 1998. She is never content to leave a quilt in its simplest form; she's always looking for ideas to make it more interesting. Finding new ways to set a quilt fascinates her.

Avis Shirer and Tammy Johnson

"Fresh Flowers," page 48

Avis and Tammy both grew up in rural, northern Iowa where they enjoyed four distinct seasons. Their favorite quilts are seasonal ones. Tammy enjoys winter; she loves Christmas, and snowmen are her favorite. Avis adores Halloween as well as anything with flowers. They consider themselves fortunate that they enjoy different seasonal themes; that way the entire year is covered.

Putting together unexpected color combinations adds a bit of whimsy to their folk-art designs, and they don't stop with color. They love to combine flannels with wovens, and often embellish with velveteen, wool, buttons, or rickrack.

Since they are two friends who thoroughly enjoy each other's company, they named their pattern business Joined at the Hip. This quilt is from their first book, *Alphabet Soup.*

Evelyn Sloppy

"Anniversary Stars," page 9

This quilt is from Evelyn's most recent book, *40 Fabulous Quick-Cut Quilts.* Her previous books include *Log Cabin Fever* and *Frayed-Edge Fun.*

Evelyn has been quilting since 1991. Her favorites are scrappy, traditional quilts, but she also enjoys trying new ideas and stretching her imagination. She loves using new techniques that make quiltmaking faster, more accurate, and just more fun. Although she appreciates hand quilting, she finishes most of her quilts on her long-arm quilting machine. Evelyn enjoys country living in western Washington and loves to travel and hike.

Mary Sue Suit

"Holiday Topper," page 76

Mary Sue is a self-taught quiltmaker whose love of geometric designs led her to develop her own techniques and tools for creating patchwork quilts. This quilt is from her most recent book, *Crazy Eights.* Her work has also been featured in several quilt magazines and on the television show *Simply Quilts.*

Cynthia Tomaszewski

"Sweet Dreams," page 60

Cynthia learned to sew at the age of 10 and has been quilting since 1982. This quilt is from her second book, *Tea in the Garden.* Her first book was *Garden Party.* Cynthia's passions are quilting, appliqué quilts in particular, and travel, especially among exotic cultures. She believes it's the simple things in life that bring us the most pleasure. She hand pieces most of her designs and hand quilts as many as time allows.

Cynthia operates her quilt design company, Simple Pleasures, from offices in Michigan and Abu Dhabi, United Arab Emirates, where she currently resides.

Kathleen Tracy

"Underground Railroad," page 36, and "Civil War Nine Patch," page 40

Kathleen began her quilting career by making quilts for her daughter's dolls and bears. Small quilts with an antique look fascinated her, and she began designing her own patterns in the colors she loved. Kathleen started her own pattern and quilt-kit business, Country Lane Quilts, to give new quilters the convenience of simple design and old-fashioned fabrics combined. These quilts are from her first book, *American Doll Quilts*.